Ashton's memorial: or, an authentick account of the strange adventures and signal deliverances of Mr. Philip Ashton; who, after he had made his escape from the pirates

Philip Ashton

Ashton's memorial: or, an authentick account of the strange adventures and signal deliverances of Mr. Philip Ashton; who, after he had made his escape from the pirates, liv'd alone on a desolate island for about 16 months, &c. With a short account of Mr.
Ashton, Philip, Mr.
ESTCID: T142948
Reproduction from British Library
The narratives of Ashton and Merritt are in the first person and were written by Mr Barnard from their own verbal accounts.
London : printed for Richard Ford and Samuel Chandler, 1726.
148p. ; 12°

Eighteenth Century
Collections Online
Print Editions

Gale ECCO Print Editions

Relive history with *Eighteenth Century Collections Online*, now available in print for the independent historian and collector. This series includes the most significant English-language and foreign-language works printed in Great Britain during the eighteenth century, and is organized in seven different subject areas including literature and language; medicine, science, and technology; and religion and philosophy. The collection also includes thousands of important works from the Americas.

The eighteenth century has been called "The Age of Enlightenment." It was a period of rapid advance in print culture and publishing, in world exploration, and in the rapid growth of science and technology – all of which had a profound impact on the political and cultural landscape. At the end of the century the American Revolution, French Revolution and Industrial Revolution, perhaps three of the most significant events in modern history, set in motion developments that eventually dominated world political, economic, and social life.

In a groundbreaking effort, Gale initiated a revolution of its own: digitization of epic proportions to preserve these invaluable works in the largest online archive of its kind. Contributions from major world libraries constitute over 175,000 original printed works. Scanned images of the actual pages, rather than transcriptions, recreate the works *as they first appeared.*

Now for the first time, these high-quality digital scans of original works are available via print-on-demand, making them readily accessible to libraries, students, independent scholars, and readers of all ages.

For our initial release we have created seven robust collections to form one the world's most comprehensive catalogs of 18th century works.

Initial Gale ECCO Print Editions collections include:

History and Geography
Rich in titles on English life and social history, this collection spans the world as it was known to eighteenth-century historians and explorers. Titles include a wealth of travel accounts and diaries, histories of nations from throughout the world, and maps and charts of a world that was still being discovered. Students of the War of American Independence will find fascinating accounts from the British side of conflict.

Social Science

Delve into what it was like to live during the eighteenth century by reading the first-hand accounts of everyday people, including city dwellers and farmers, businessmen and bankers, artisans and merchants, artists and their patrons, politicians and their constituents. Original texts make the American, French, and Industrial revolutions vividly contemporary.

Medicine, Science and Technology

Medical theory and practice of the 1700s developed rapidly, as is evidenced by the extensive collection, which includes descriptions of diseases, their conditions, and treatments. Books on science and technology, agriculture, military technology, natural philosophy, even cookbooks, are all contained here.

Literature and Language

Western literary study flows out of eighteenth-century works by Alexander Pope, Daniel Defoe, Henry Fielding, Frances Burney, Denis Diderot, Johann Gottfried Herder, Johann Wolfgang von Goethe, and others. Experience the birth of the modern novel, or compare the development of language using dictionaries and grammar discourses.

Religion and Philosophy

The Age of Enlightenment profoundly enriched religious and philosophical understanding and continues to influence present-day thinking. Works collected here include masterpieces by David Hume, Immanuel Kant, and Jean-Jacques Rousseau, as well as religious sermons and moral debates on the issues of the day, such as the slave trade. The Age of Reason saw conflict between Protestantism and Catholicism transformed into one between faith and logic -- a debate that continues in the twenty-first century.

Law and Reference

This collection reveals the history of English common law and Empire law in a vastly changing world of British expansion. Dominating the legal field is the *Commentaries of the Law of England* by Sir William Blackstone, which first appeared in 1765. Reference works such as almanacs and catalogues continue to educate us by revealing the day-to-day workings of society.

Fine Arts

The eighteenth-century fascination with Greek and Roman antiquity followed the systematic excavation of the ruins at Pompeii and Herculaneum in southern Italy; and after 1750 a neoclassical style dominated all artistic fields. The titles here trace developments in mostly English-language works on painting, sculpture, architecture, music, theater, and other disciplines. Instructional works on musical instruments, catalogs of art objects, comic operas, and more are also included.

old books. new life.

The BiblioLife Network

This project was made possible in part by the BiblioLife Network (BLN), a project aimed at addressing some of the huge challenges facing book preservationists around the world. The BLN includes libraries, library networks, archives, subject matter experts, online communities and library service providers. We believe every book ever published should be available as a high-quality print reproduction; printed on-demand anywhere in the world. This insures the ongoing accessibility of the content and helps generate sustainable revenue for the libraries and organizations that work to preserve these important materials.

The following book is in the "public domain" and represents an authentic reproduction of the text as printed by the original publisher. While we have attempted to accurately maintain the integrity of the original work, there are sometimes problems with the original work or the micro-film from which the books were digitized. This can result in minor errors in reproduction. Possible imperfections include missing and blurred pages, poor pictures, markings and other reproduction issues beyond our control. Because this work is culturally important, we have made it available as part of our commitment to protecting, preserving, and promoting the world's literature.

GUIDE TO FOLD-OUTS MAPS and OVERSIZED IMAGES

The book you are reading was digitized from microfilm captured over the past thirty to forty years. Years after the creation of the original microfilm, the book was converted to digital files and made available in an online database.

In an online database, page images do not need to conform to the size restrictions found in a printed book. When converting these images back into a printed bound book, the page sizes are standardized in ways that maintain the detail of the original. For large images, such as fold-out maps, the original page image is split into two or more pages

Guidelines used to determine how to split the page image follows:

• Some images are split vertically; large images require vertical and horizontal splits.
• For horizontal splits, the content is split left to right.
• For vertical splits, the content is split from top to bottom.
• For both vertical and horizontal splits, the image is processed from top left to bottom right.

Ashton's *Memorial*:

Or, An Authentick

ACCOUNT

O F

The Strange Adventures and Signal Deliverances

O F

Mr. *Philip Ashton*;

W H O,

After he had made his Escape from the PIRATES, liv'd alone on a desolate Island for about 16 Months, &c.

With a short Account of

Mr. NICHOLAS MERRITT,

who was taken at the same time.

To which is added,

A SERMON on *Dan.* iii. 17

By JOHN BARNARD, *V. D. M.*

—— *We should not trust in our selves, but in God*
—— *who delivered us from so great a Death, and doth*
deliver, in whom we trust, that he will yet deli-
ver us. 2 Cor. i. 9, 10.

LONDON:
Printed for RICHARD FORD and SAMUEL
CHANDLER, both in the *Poultry*. 1726.

TO THE
READER.

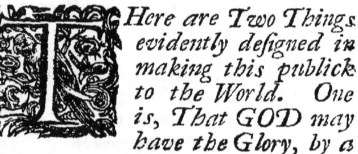

THere are Two Things
evidently defigned in
making this publick
to the World. One
is, That GOD may
have the Glory, by a
grateful Remembrance, and thankful Acknowledgment of his Power
and Goodnefs, in his wonderful
Works to the Children of Men. For
fuch remarkable Inftances are a
clear Teftimony to the Superintendency of fome Supream Power, and
All-wife Agent over the Kingdom of
Providence, who has the fole Government of all fecondary Caufes,
and gives unexpected and furprizing
turns and Changes both to the
Hearts

Hearts and Affairs of Mankind ; and who is therefore ever to be acknowledged by us in all our Ways, and worshipped with a Religious Fear and Reverence.

The other is, That all Men may be led to a steady Hope and Trust in that GOD, whose Eyes run to and fro in the Earth, beholding the Evil and the Good, that he may shew himself strong on the Behalf of those whose Hearts are perfect towards him; that their Minds being fortified with the firm Belief of the governing Providence of GOD, and his Ability to do more than they can ask or think, may secure them against running into those irregular Methods to obtain Relief under the melancholy Prospect of approaching Want, to free themselves from any present Burdens, or to escape any threatning Danger, into which their prevailing, but misguided Fears may be apt to hurry them.

More particularly, that those whose Business lies upon the great
Waters

Waters, and especially our Fishing-Tribe (if ever it should be the unhappy Portion of any of them to fall into the Hands of the Sons of Violence, which GOD prevent!) may learn from hence, that it is safer trusting GOD, than Man, with the Disposal of their Lives; and that therefore it will be their wisest Course to take up sober Resolutions, utterly to refuse all sinful Compliances with them in their pernicious Practices, let their Threatnings of immediate-Death be ever so fiercely repeated, seeing the Infinitely Wise GOD has unknown Methods to preserve and deliver them; rather than by willingly associating themselves with them in their evil Manners, to forfeit the Protection of Heaven, and unavoidably rush into that Misery and Death which they vainly think to escape.

The great Reason why this Narrative, which has been so long wished for, has no sooner appeared, is, because Mr. Ashton has necessarily

A 3

been

been *so much absent*, that I have not been able to get the Opportunity of conferring with him more than two or three times, about the remarkable Occurrences he has met with; and having had no Leisure himself to write, I have taken the Minutes of all from his own Mouth, and after I had put them together, I have improved the first vacant Hour I could to read it over distinctly to him, that he might correct the Errors that might arise from my misunderstanding his Report. Thus corrected, he has set his Hand to it as his own History.

I have added to it a short Account of Mr. Nicholas Merritt, who was taken at the same time with Mr. Ashton, the Manner of his Escape from the Pirates, and the hard Usage he met with upon it, till his Return to his own Country, which I had from his own Mouth, all tending to the same End and Purpose.

I would

I would only add, that I have too great an Opinion of the Virtue of both the Persons mentioned (and so, I think, have all that know them) to suppose they would in the least entertain the World with Fables instead of Realities.

And if the great Ends hereof, the Glory of GOD, and the Good of Mankind, may be in any measure promoted hereby, (which GOD grant) I shall not think much of the Time and Pains I have taken in Writing it.

Marble-Head,
Aug. 3. 1725.

J. Barnard.

Ashton's *Memorial:*

Or, An Authentick
ACCOUNT
OF
The Strange Adventures and Signal Deliverances
OF
Mr. PHIL. ASHTON, *jun.*
of *Marble-Head.*

UPON *Friday,* *June* 15th, 1722. after I had been out for some time in the Schooner *Milton,* upon the Fishing-Grounds off *Cape-Sable* Shoar, among others I came to sail in Company with *Nicholas Merritt* in a Shallop, and stood in for *Port-Rossaway,* designing to harbour
bour

bour there till the Sabbath was over, where we arriv'd about 4 o'Clock in the Afternoon. When we came into the Harbour, where several of our Fishing-Vessels had arriv'd before us, we spy'd among them a Brigantine, which we suppos'd to have been an inward-bound Vessel from the *West Indies,* and had no Apprehensions of any Danger from her; but by that time we had been at Anchor two or three Hours, a Boat from the Brigantine, with four Hands, came along-side of us, and the Men jump'd in upon our Deck, without our suspecting any thing but that they were Friends come on board to visit, or inquire what News; till they drew their Curtlasses and Pistols from under their Cloaths, and cock'd the one, and brandish'd the other, and began to curse and swear at us, and demanded a Surrender of our selves and Vessel to them. It was too late for us to rectify our Mistake, and think of freeing our selves from their Power: For however we might have been able (being five of us and a Boy) to have kept them at a Distance, had we known who they were before they had boarded us; yet now we had our Arms to seek, and being in no Capacity to make any Resistance, were

were neceffitated to fubmit our felves to their Will and Pleafure. In this man-ner they furprized *Nicholas Merritt* and twelve or thirteen other Fifhing-Veffels this Evening.

When the Boat went off from our Veffel, they carried me on board the Brigantine, and who fhould it prove but the infamous *Ned Low* the Pirate, with about 42 Hands, 2 Great Guns, and 4 Swivel-Guns. You may eafily imagine how I look'd and felt, when, too late to prevent it, I found my felf fallen into the Hands of fuch a mad, roaring, mifchievous Crew; yet I hop'd that they would not force me away with them, and I purpofed to endure any Hardfhip among them patiently, rather than turn Pirate with them.

Low prefently fent for me Aft, and according to the Pirates ufual Cuftom, and in their proper Dialect, asked me, *If I would fign their Articles, and go along with them.* I told him, *No;* I could by no means confent to go with them; I fhould be glad if he would give me my Liberty, and put me on board any Veffel, or fet me on Shoar there. For indeed my Diflike of their Company and Actions, my Concern for my Pa-rents, and my Fears of being found in

fuch

such bad Company, made me dread the Thoughts of being carried away by them; so that I had not the least Inclination to continue with them.

Upon my utter Refusal to join and go with them, I was thrust down into the Hold, which I found to be a safe Retreat for me several times afterward. By that time I had been in the Hold a few Hours, they had compleated the taking the several Vessels that were in the Harbour, and the examining of the Men; and the next Day I was fetched up with some others that were there, and about 30 or 40 of us were put on board a Schooner belonging to Mr. *Orn* of *Marble-Head,* which the Pirates made use of for a sort of Prison upon the present Occasion, where we were all confin'd unarm'd, with an armed Guard over us, till the *Sultan*'s Pleasure should be further known.

The next Lord's Day about Noon, one of the Quarter-Masters, *John Russel* by Name, came on board the Schooner, and took six of us, *Nicholas Merritt, Joseph Libbie, Lawrence Fabins,* and *my self,* all of *Marble-Head* (the eldest of us, if I mistake not, under 21 Years of Age) with two others, and carried us on board the Brigantine, where we were
called

called upon the Quarter-Deck, and *Low* came up to us with Piftol in hand, and with a full Mouth demanded, *Are any of you married Men?* This fhort and un-expected Queftion, and the Sight of the Piftol, ftruck us all dumb, and not a Man of us dared to fpeak a Word, for fear there fhould have been a Defign in it, which we were not able to fee thro'. Our Silence kindled our new Mafter into a Flame, who could not bear it that fo many beardlefs Boys fhould de-ny him an Anfwer to fo plain a Que-ftion; and therefore, in a Rage, he cock'd his Piftol, and clapt it to my Head, and cried out, *You D-g! why don't you anfwer me?* and fwore vehemently, he would fhoot me thro' the Head if I did not tell him immediately whether I was married or no.

I was fufficiently frightned at the Fiercenefs of the Man, and the Bold-nefs of his Threatning, but rather than lofe my Life, for fo trifling a Matter, I even ventur'd at length to tell him, *I was not married,* (as loud as I dar'd to fpeak it;) and fo faid the reft of my Companions Upon this he feemed fomething pacified, and turned away from us.

B It

It seems his Design was to take no married Man away with him, how young foever he might be, which I often wonder'd at, till after I had been with him fome confiderable Time, and could obferve in him an Uneafinefs in the Sentiments of his Mind, and the Workings of his Paffions towards a young Child he had at *Bofton* (his Wife being dead, as I learned, fome fmall Time before he turned Pirate) which (upon every lucid Interval from Revelling and Drink) he would exprefs a great Tendernefs for, infomuch that I have feen him fit down and weep plentifully upon the mentioning of it ; and then I concluded, that probably the Reafon of his taking none but fingle Men was, that he might have none with him under the Influence of fuch powerful Attractives as a Wife and Children, left they fhould grow uneafy in his Service, and have an Inclination to defert him, and return home for the Sake of their Families.

Low prefently came up to us again, and asked the old Queftion, Whether we would fign their Articles, and go along with them ? We all told him no ; we could not ; fo we were difmiffed. But within a little while we were call'd to him fingly, and then it was demanded

of

of me, with Sternnefs and Threats, whether I would join with them? I ftill perfifted in the Denial, which (thro' the Affiftance of Heaven) I was refolved to do, tho' he fhot me; and, as I underftood, all my fix Companions, who were called in their Turns, ftill refufed to go with him.

Then I was led down into the Steerage, by one of the Quarter-Mafters, and there I was affaulted with Temptations of another kind, in hopes to win me over to become one of them; a number of 'em got about me, and, inftead of Hiffing, fhook their Rattles, and treated me with abundance of Refpect and Kindnefs in their Way; they did all they could to footh my Sorrows, and fet before me the ftrong Allurement of the vaft Riches they fhould gain, and what mighty Men they defigned to be, and would fain have me to join with 'em and fhare in their Spoils; and to make all go down the more glib, they greatly importuned me to drink with them, not doubting but this Wile would fufficiently entangle me, and fo they fhould prevail with me to do that in my Cups, which they perceived they could not bring me to while I was fober; but all their fair and plaufible Carriage, their

B 2   proffer-

proffered Kindnefs, and airy Notions of Riches, had not the Effect upon me which they defired; and I had no Inclination to drown my Sorrows with my Senfes in their inebriating Bowls, and fo refufed their Drink as well as their Propofals.

After this, I was brought upon Deck again, and *Low* came up to me with his Piftol cock'd, and clapt it to my Head, and faid to me, *You D-g you! if you will not fign our Articles, and go along with me, I'll fhoot you thro' the Head*; and uttered his Threats with his utmoft Fiercenefs, and with the ufual Flafhes of Swearing and Curfing   I told him, *That I was in his Hands, and he might do with me what he pleafed, but I could not be willing to go with him*; and then I earneftly begg'd of him, with many Tears, and ufed all the Arguments I could think of to perfwade him not to carry me away; but he was deaf to my Cries, and unmoved by all I could fay to him, and told me, *I was an impudent D-g,* and fwore, *I fhould go with him whether I would or no.* So I found all my Cries and Entreaties were in vain, and there was no Help for it, go with them I muft, and, as I underftood, they fet mine and my Townfmens Names down in their Book, tho' againft our Confent.   And I defire to
mention

mention it with due Acknowledgments to God, who withheld me, that neither their Promises, nor their Threatnings, nor Blows, could move me to a Willingness to join with them in their pernicious Ways.

Upon *Tuesday, June* 19, they changed their Vessel, and took for their Privateer (as they call'd it) a Schooner belonging to Mr. *Joseph Dolliber* of *Marble-Head*, being new, clean, and a good Sailer, and shipped all their Hands on board her, and put the Prisoners (such as they designed to send home) on board the Brigantine, with one ——— who was her Master, and ordered them for *Boston*.

When I saw the Captives were likely to be sent home, I thought I would make one Attempt more to obtain my Freedom, and accordingly *Nicholas Merritt*, my Townsman and Kinsman, went along with me to *Low*, and we fell upon our Knees, and with the utmost Importunity besought him to let us go home in the Brigantine, among the rest of the Captives; but he immediately called for his Pistols, and told us we should not go, and swore bitterly, if either of us offered to stir, he would shoot us down.

Thus

Thus all Attempts to be delivered out of the Hands of unreasonable Men, (if they may be called Men) were hitherto unsuccessful, and I had the melancholy Prospect of seeing the Brigantine sail away with the most of us that were taken at *Port-Rossaway*, but my self, and three Townsmen mentioned, and four *Isle of Shoal* Men, detained on board the Schooner, in the worst of Captivity, without any present Likelihood of escaping.

And yet before the Brigantine sailed, an Opportunity presented, that gave me some Hopes that I might get away from them; for some of *Low*'s People, who had been on Shoar at *Port-Rossaway* to get Water, had left a Dog belonging to him behind them; and *Low* observing the Dog a-shoar, howling to come off, order'd some Hands to take the Boat and fetch him. Two young Men, *John Holman*, and *Benjamin Ashton*, both of *Marble-Head*, readily jumpt into the Boat, and I, (who pretty well knew their Inclination to be rid of such Company, and was exceedingly desirous my self to be freed from my present Station, and thought if I could but once set foot on Shoar, they should have good Luck to get me on board again)

gain) was getting over the Side into the Boat; but Quarter-Master *Ruſſel* ſpy'd me, and caught hold on my Shoulder, and drew me in board, and with a Curſe told me, Two was enough, I ſhould not go. The two young Men had more Senſe and Virtue than to come off to them again, ſo that after ſome time of waiting, they found they were deprived of their Men, their Boat, and their Dog; and they could not go after them.

When they ſaw what a Trick was play'd them, the Quarter-Master came up to me curſing and ſwearing, that I knew of their Deſign to run away, and intended to have been one of them; (but tho' it would have been an unſpeakable Pleaſure to me to have been with them, yet) I was forced to tell him, I knew not of their Deſign; and indeed I did not, tho' I had good Reaſon to ſuſpect what would be the Event of their going. This did not pacify the Quarter-Master, who with outragious Curſing and Swearing clapt his Piſtol to my Head, and ſnap'd it, but it miſs'd Fire. This enraged him the more, and he repeated the ſnapping of his Piſtol at my Head three times, and it as often miſs'd Fire; upon which he held it over-board, and ſnap'd it the fourth time, and then it went off

very

very readily. (Thus did God mercifully quench the Violence of the Fire that was meant to deftroy me!) The Quarter-Mafter, upon this, in the utmoft Fury, drew his Cutlafh, and fell upon me with it, but I leap'd down into the Hold, and got among a Crowd that was there, and fo efcaped the further Effects of his Madnefs and Rage. Thus, tho' GOD fuffer'd me not to gain my wifh'd-for Freedom, yet he wonderfully preferv'd me from Death.

All Hopes of obtaining Deliverance were now paft and gone, the Brigantine and Fifhing-Veffels were now upon their Way homeward, the Boat was afhore, and not likely to come off again; I could fee no poffible Way of Efcape; and who can exprefs the Concern and Agony I was in, to fee my felf, a young Lad, not twenty Years old, carried forcibly from my Parents, (whom I had fo much Reafon to value for the Tendernefs I knew they had for me, and to whom, my being among Pirates, would be as a Sword in their Bowels, and the Anguifhes of Death to them) confined to fuch Company as I could not but have an exceeding great Abhorrence of; in Danger of being poifoned in my Morals, by living among them, and of falling a
Sacrifice

Sacrifice to Juftice, if ever I fhould be taken with them. I had no way left for my Comfort, but earneftly to commit my felf and my Caufe to God, and wait upon him for Deliverance in his own Time and Way; and in the mean while firmly to refolve, through Divine Affiftance, that nothing fhould ever bring me to a Willingnefs to join with them, or fhare in their Spoils.

I foon found, that any Death was preferable to being link'd with fuch a vile Crew of Mifcreants, to whom it was a Sport to do Mifchief; where prodigious Drinking, monftrous Curfing and Swearing, hideous Blafphemies, and open Defiance of Heaven, and Contempt of Hell it felf, was the conftant Employment, unlefs when Sleep fomething abated the Noife and Revellings.

Thus confined, the beft Courfe I could take was to keep out of the Way down in the Hold, or wherever I could be moft free from their perpetual Din; and fixedly purpofe with my felf, that the firft time I had an Opportunity to fet my Foot on Shore, let it be in what Part of the World it would, it fhould prove (if poffible) my taking a final Leave of *Low* and Company.

E

I would remark it now also (that I might not interrupt the Story with it afterwards) that while I was on board *Low*, they used once a Week or Fortnight, as the Evil Spirit moved them, to bring me under Examination, and anew demand my signing their Articles, and joining with them; but (blessed be God) I was enabled to persist in a constant Refusal to become one of them, tho' I was thrash'd with Sword or Cane as often as I denied them; the Fury of which I had no way to avoid, but by jumping down into the Hold, where for a while I was safe. I looked upon my self for a long while but as a dead Man among them, and expected every Day of Examination would prove the last of my Life, till I learned from some of them, that it was one of their Articles, Not to draw Blood, or take away the Life of any Man, after they had given him Quarter, unless he was to be punished as a Criminal; and this embolden'd me afterwards, so that I was not so much afraid to deny them, seeing my Life was given me for a Prey.

This *Tuesday*, towards Evening, *Low* and Company came to sail in the Schooner formerly called the *Mary*, now the *Fancy*, and made off for *Newfoundland;*
and

and here they met with fuch an Adventure as had like to have proved fatal to them. They fell in with the Mouth of St. *John's* Harbour in a Fog before they knew where they were, when the Fog clearing up a little, they fpy'd a large Ship riding at Anchor in the Harbour, but could not difcern what fhe was by reafon of the Thicknefs of the Air, and concluded fhe was a Fifh-Trader; this they look'd upon as a boon Prize for them, and thought they hould be wonderfully well accommodated with a good Ship under Foot, and if fhe proved but a good Sailer, would greatly further their roving Defigns, and render them a Match for almoft any thing they could meet with, fo that they need not fear being taken.

Accordingly they came to a Refolution to go in and take her; and imagining it was beft doing it by Stratagem, they concluded to put all their Hands but fix or feven down in the Hold, and make a Shew as if they were a Fifhing-Veffel, and fo run up along-fide of her, and furprize her, and bring her off; and great was their Joy at the diftant Profpect how cleverly they fhould catch her. They began to put their Defigns in Execution, ftow'd away their

Hands,

Hands, leaving but a few upon Deck, and made Sail in order to seize the Prey; when there comes along a small Fisher-Boat from out the Harbour, and hail'd them, and ask'd them from whence they were; they told them, from *Barbadoes*, and were laden with Rhum and Sugar. Then they ask'd the Fisherman what large Ship that was in the Harbour; who told them it was a large Man of War.

The very Name of a Man of War struck them all up in a Heap, spoiled their Mirth, their fair Hopes, and promising Design of having a good Ship at Command; and, left they should catch a Tartar, they thought it their wisest and safest Way, instead of going into the Harbour, to be gone as fast as they could; and accordingly they stretched away farther Eastward, and put into a small Harbour call'd *Carboneur*, about 15 Leagues Distance; where they went on Shoar, took the Place, and destroyed the Houses, but hurt none of the People, as they told me, for I was not suffered to go ashoar with them.

The next Day they made off for the *Grand Bank*, where they took seven or eight Vessels, and among them a *French* Banker, a Ship of about 350 Tons and 2 Guns;

2 Guns; this they carried off with them, and stood away for St. *Michael's.*

Off of St. *Michael's* they took a large *Portugueze* Pink, laden with Wheat, coming out of the Road, which I was told was formerly called the *Rose Frigat.* She struck to the Schooner, fearing the large Ship that was coming down to them; tho' all *Low's* Force had been no Match for her, if the *Portugueze* had made a good Resistance. This Pink they soon observ'd to be a much better Sailer than their *French* Banker, which went heavily, and therefore they threw the greatest Part of the Wheat over-board, reserving only enough to ballast the Vessel for the present, and took what they wanted out of the Banker, and then burnt her, and sent most of the *Portugueze* away in a large Lanch they had taken.

Now they made the Pink, which mounted 14 Guns, their Commodore, and with this and the Schooner sailed from St *Michael's* to the *Canaries,* where off of *Teneriff,* they gave Chace to a Sloop, which got under the Command of the Fortress, and so escaped falling into their Hands; but stretching along to the Western End of the Island, they came up with a Fishing-Boat, and be-

C ing

ing in Want of Water, made them pilot them into a small Harbour, where they went a-shore and got a Supply.

After they had watered, they sailed away for *Cape de Verde* Islands, and upon making the Isle of *May*, they descry'd a Sloop, which they took, and it proved to be a *Bristol*-Man, one *Pare* or *Pier*, Master; this Sloop they designed for a Tender, and put on board her my Kinsman *Nicholas Merritt*, with eight or nine Hands more, and sailed away for *Bonavista*, with a Design to careen their Vessels.

In their Passage to *Bonavista*, the Sloop wronged both the Pink and the Schooner; which the Hands on board observing, being mostly forced Men, or such as were weary of their Employment, upon the fifth of *September* ran away with her, and made their Escape.

When they came to *Bonavista*, they hove down the Schooner, and careen'd her, and then the Pink, and here they gave the Wheat, which they had kept to ballast the Pink with, to the *Portugueze*, and took other Ballast.

After they had clean'd and fitted their Vessels, they steered away for *St. Nicholas*, to get better Water; and here, as I was told, seven or eight Hands

out

out of the Pink went afhore a Fowling, but never came off more, among which I fuppofe *Lawrence Fabins* was one ; and what became of them, I could never hear to this Day. Then they put out to Sea, and ftood away for the Coaft of *Brafil*, hoping to meet with richer Pri- es than they had yet taken. In the Paffage thither, they made a Ship, which they gave Chace to, but could not come up with ; and when they came upon the Coaft, it had like to have proved a bad Coaft to them ; for the Trade-Winds blowing exceeding hard at South Eaft, they fell in upon the northern Part of the Coaft, near 200 Leagues to the Lee- ward of where they defigned ; and here we were all in exceeding great Danger, and for five Days and Nights together hourly feared when we fhould be fwal- lowed up by the Violence of the Wind and Sea, or ftranded upon fome of the fhoals, that lay many Leagues off from Land. In this Time of Extremity, the poor Wretches had no where to go for Help, for they were at open Defiance with their Maker, and they could have but little Comfort in the Thoughts of their Agreement with Hell ; such migh- y Hectors as they were in a clear Sky and a fair Gale, yet a fierce Wind and a boisterous Sea funk their Spirits to a cowardly Dejection, and they evidently feared the Almighty, whom before they defied, left He was come to torment them before their expected Time. And tho' they were fo habituated to Curfing and Swearing, that the difmal Profpect of Death, and this of fo long Continuance, could not correct the Language of moft of them, yet you might plainly fee the inward Horror and Anguifh of their Minds, vifible in their Countenances, and like Men amazed, or ftarting out of Sleep in a Fright, I could hear them every now and then cry out, *Oh! I wifh I were at Home!*

When the Fiercenefs of the Weather was over, and they had recovered their Spirits, by the Help of a little *Nantes*, they bore away to the *Weft-Indies*, and made the three Iflands call'd the *Triangles*, lying off the Main about 40 Leagues to the Eaftward of *Surinam*. Here they went in and careened their Veffels again, and it had like to have proved a fatal Scouring to them.

For as they hove down the Pink, *Low* had ordered fo many Hands upon the Shrowds and Yards, to throw her Bottom out of Water, that it threw her Ports, which were open, under Water, and

and the Water flow'd in with such
Freedom that it presently overset her.
Low and the Doctor were in the Cabin together, and as soon as he perceived the Water to gush in upon him, he bolted out at one of the
Stern-Ports, which the Doctor also attempted, but the Sea rushed so violent-
ly into the Port by that time, as to
force him back into the Cabin, upon
which *Low* nimbly run his Arm into
the Port, and caught hold of his Shoulder, and drew him out, and so saved
him. The Vessel pitched her Masts to
the Ground, in about 6 Fathom Water,
and turn'd her Keel out of Water; but
as her Hull fill'd, it sunk, and by the
Help of her Yard-Arms, which I sup-
ose bore upon the Ground, her Masts
were raised something out of Water; the
Men that were upon her Shrowds and
Yards got upon her Hull, when that was
uppermost, and then upon her Top-Masts
and Shrowds, when they were raised a-
gain. I (who with other light Lads
were sent up to the Main-Top-Gallant
Yard) was very difficultly put to it to
save my Life, being but a poor Swim-
ner; for the Boat which pick'd the
Men up refused to take me in, and I
was put upon making the best of my

way to the Buoy, which with much a-do I recovered, and it being large, I ftayed my felf by it, till the Boat came along clofe by it, and then I called to 'em to take me in; but they being full of Men, ftill refufed me; and I did not know but they meant to leave me to perifh there; but the Boat making way a-head very flowly, becaufe of her deep Load, and *Jofeph Libbie* calling to me to put off from the Buoy and fwim to them, I e'en ventur'd it, and he took me by the Hand and drew me on board. They loft two Men by this Accident, *viz. John Bell,* and one they called *Zana Gourdon.* The Men that were on board the Schooner were bufy a mending the Sails, under an Auning, fo they knew nothing of what had happened to the Pink, till the Boat full of Men came along-fide of 'em, (tho' they were but about Gun-fhot off, and we made a great Out-cry,) and therefore they fent not their Boat to help take up the Men.

And now *Low* and his Gang having loft their Frigate, and with her the greateft part of their Provifion and Water, were again reduced to their Schooner, as their only Privateer, and in her they put to Sea, and were brought to very

very great Straights for want of Water; for they could not get a Supply at the *Triangles*, and when they hoped to furnish themselves at *Tabago*, the Current set so strong, and the Season was so calm, that they could not recover the Harbour, so they were forced to stand away for *Grand Grenada*, a French Island about 18 Leagues to the Westward of *Tabago*, which they gained, after they had been at the Hardship of half a Pint of Water a Man for sixteen Days together.

Here the *French* came on board, and *Low* having put all his Men down, but a sufficient Number to sail the Vessel, told them upon their Enquiry whence he was, that he was come from *Barbadoes*, and had lost his Water, and was obliged to put in for a Recruit. The poor People not suspecting him for a Pirate, readily suffered him to send his Men ashoar, and fetch off a Supply. But the *Frenchmen* afterwards imagining he was a Smugling Trader, thought to have made a Boon Prize of him, and the next Day fitted out a large *Rhode-Island* built Sloop of 70 Tons, with 4 Guns mounted, and about 30 Hands, with Design to have taken him. *Low* was apprehensive of no Danger from them,

them, till they came close along side of him, and plainly discovered their Design by their Number and Actions, and then he called up his Hands upon Deck, and having about 90 Hands on board, and 8 Guns mounted, the Sloop and *Frenchmen* fell an easy Prey to him, and he made a Privateer of her.

After this they cruised for some time thro' the *West Indies,* in which Excursion they took 7 or 8 Sail of Vessels, chiefly Sloops; at length they came to *Santa Cruz,* where they took two Sloops more, and then came to Anchor off the Island.

While they lay at Anchor here, it came into *Low*'s Head, that he wanted a Doctor's Chest, and in order to procure one, he put four of the *Frenchmen* on board one of the Sloops which he had just now taken, and sent them away to St. *Thomas*'s (about 12 Leagues off, where the Sloops belonged) with the Promise, that if they would presently send him off a good Doctor's Chest for what he sent to purchase it with, they should have their Men and Vessels again, but if not, he would kill all the Men and burn the Vessels. The poor People, in Compassion to their Neighbours, and to preserve their Interest, readily complied with his Demands; so that in little
tle

tle more than 24 Hours the four *Frenchmen* returned with what they went for, and then, according to Promise, they and their Sloops were difmifs'd.

From *Santa Cruz* they failed till they made *Curacao*, in which Paffage they gave Chace to two Sloops that out-failed them and got clear; then they ranged the Coaft of *New-Spain*, and made *Carthagena*, and about mid-way between *Carthagena* and *Port-Abella*, they defcry'd two tall Ships, which proved to be the *Mermaid* Man of War, and a large *Guinea*-Man. *Low* was now in the *Rhode Ifland* Sloop, and one *Farrington Spriggs*, a Quarter-Mafter, was Commander of the Schooner where I ftill was. For fome time they made Sail after the two Ships, till they came fo near that they could plainly fee the Man of War's large Range of Teeth, and then they turned Tail to, and made the beft of their Way from them; upon which the Man of War gave them Chace, and overhaled them apace. And now I confefs I was in as great Terror as ever I had been yet, for I concluded we fhould be taken, and I could expect no other but to die for Company's fake; fo true is what *Solomon* tells us, *a Companion of Fools fhall be deftroyed.* But the

Pirates

Pirates finding the Man of War to over-hale them, feparated, and *Low* ftood out to Sea, and *Spriggs* ftood in for the Shoar. The Man of War obferving the Sloop to be the larger Veffel much, and fulleft of Men, threw out all the Sail fhe could, and ftood after her, and was in a fair way of coming up with her prefently ; but it happen'd there was one Man on board the Sloop that knew of a Shoal-Ground thereabouts, who directed *Low* to run over it ; he did fo, and the Man of War, (who had now fo fore-reached him as to fling a fhot over him) in the clofe Purfuit, ran a-ground upon the Shoal, and fo *Low* and Company efcaped hanging for this Time.

Spriggs, who was in the Schooner, when he faw the Danger they were in of being taken, upon the Man of War's out-failing them, was afraid of falling into the Hands of Juftice ; to prevent which, he, and one of his chief Compani-ons, took their Piftols, and laid them down by them, and folemnly fwore to each other, and pledg'd the Oath in a Bum-per of Liquor, that if they faw there was at laft no Poffibility of efcaping, but that they fhould be taken, they would fet Foot to Foot and fhoot one

another,

another, to escape Justice and the Halter. As if Divine Justice were not as inexorable as human!

But, as I said, he stood in for the Shoar, and made into *Pickeroon* Bay, about 18 Leagues from *Carthagena,* and so got out of the Reach of Danger. By this Means the Sloop and Schooner were parted, and *Spriggs* made sail towards the Bay of *Honduras,* and came to Anchor in a small Island called *Utilla,* about 7 or 8 Leagues to Leeward of *Roatan,* where (by the Help of a small Sloop he had taken the Day before) he haled down, and cleaned the Schooner.

While *Spriggs* lay at *Utilla,* there was an Opportunity presented, which gave Occasion to several of us to form a Design of making our Escape out of the Pirates Company; for having lost *Low,* and being but weak handed, *Spriggs* had determined to go thro' the Gulf, and come upon the Coast of *New-England,* to encrease his Company, and supply himself with Provision; whereupon a Number of us had enter'd into a Combination to take the first fair Advantage to subdue our Masters, and free our selves. There were in all about 24 Men on board the Schooner, and

and 8 of us were in the Plot, which was, That when we fhould come upon the Coaft of *New-England*, we would take the Opportunity, when the Crew had fufficiently dozed themfelves with Drink, and had got found afleep, to fecure them under the Hatches, and bring the Veffel and Company in, and throw our felves upon the Mercy of the Government.

But it pleafed G O D to difappoint our Defign The Day that they came to fail out of *Utilla*, after they had been parted from *Low* about five Weeks, they difcovered a large Sloop, which bore down upon them. *Spriggs*, who knew not the Sloop, but imagined it might be a *Spanifh* Privateer, full of Men, being but weak handed himfelf, made the beft of his Way from her. The Sloop greatly overhaled the Schooner. *Low*, who knew the Schooner, and thought that fince they had been feparated fhe might have fallen into the Hands of ho- neft Men, fired upon her, and ftruck her the fii ft Shot. *Spriggs*, feeing the Sloop fuller of Men than ordinary, (for *Low* had been to *Honduras*, and had ta- ken a Sloop, and brought off feve- ral *Baymen*, and was now become an Hundred ftrong) and remaining ftill ig-

norant of his old Mate, refused to bring
to, but continued to make off, and refolved, if they came up with him, to
fight them the beft he could. Thus the
Harpies had like to have fallen foul of
one another. But *Low* hoifting his Pirate Colours, difcovered who he was;
and then, hideous was the noify Joy
among the piratical Crew, on all Sides,
accompanied with Firing and Carou-
fing, at the finding their old Mafter and
Companions, and their narrow Efcape;
and fo the Defign of crufing upon the
Coaft of *New-England* came to nothing.
A good Providence it was to my dear
Country that it did fo, unlefs we could
have timely fucceeded in our Defign to
furprize them.

Yet it had like to have proved a fatal
Providence to thofe of us that had a
Hand in the Plot; for tho' our Defign
f furprifing *Spriggs* and Company when
we fhould come upon the Coaft of *New-
England* was carry'd with as much Se-
recy as poffible, (we hardly daring to
truft one another, and mentioning it
always with the utmoft Privacy, and
not plainly, but in diftant Hints) yet
now that *Low* appeared, *Spriggs* had got
an Account of it fome Way or other;
and full of Refentment and Rage he

D   goes

goes a-board *Low,* and acquaints him with what he called our treacherous Defign, and fays all he can to provoke him to revenge the Mifchief upon us, and earneftly urged that we might be fhot. But GOD (who has the Hearts of all Men in his own Hands, and turns them as he pleafes) fo over-ruled, that *Low* turn'd it off with a Laugh, and faid he did not know, but if it had been his own Cafe, as it was ours, he fhould have done fo himfelf; and all that *Spriggs* could fay was not able to ftir up his Refentments, and procure any heavy Sentence upon us.

Thus *Low's* merry Air faved us at that time; for had he lifped a Word in compliance with what *Spriggs* urged, we had furely fome of us, if not all, have been loft. Upon this he comes on board the Schooner again, heated with Drink, but more chafed in his own Mind, that he could not have his Will of us, and fwore and tore like a Mad-man, crying out, That four of us ought to go forward, and be fhot; and to me in particular he faid, *You D-g, Afh-*ton, *deferve to be hang'd up at the Yard Arm, for defigning to cut us off.* I told him, I had no Defign of hurting any Man on board, but if they would

m

me go away quietly, I should be glad. This Matter made a very great Noise on board for several Hours, but at length the Fire was quenched, and, thro' the Goodness of GOD, I escaped being consumed by the Violence of the Flame.

The next Day, *Low* ordered all into *Roatan* Harbour to clean; and here it was, that thro' the Favour of GOD to me, I first gained Deliverance out of the Pirates Hands; tho' it was a long while before my Deliverance was perfected, in a Return to my Country and Friends, as you will see in the Sequel.

Roatan Harbour, as all about the Gulf of *Honduras*, is full of small Islands, which go by the general Name of the Keys. When we had got in here, *Low* and some of his chief Men had got ashore upon one of these small Islands, which they called *Port-Royal Key*, where they made them Booths, and were Carousing, Drinking and Firing, while the two Sloops, the *Rhode-Island*, and that which Low brought with him from the Bay, were cleaning As for the Schooner, he loaded her with the Logwood which the Sloop brought from the Bay, and gave her, according to Promise, to one *John Blaze*, and put four Men along with him in her, and when they came to fail from this Place, fent them away upon their own Account, and what became of them, I know not.

Upon *Saturday,* the 9th of *March,* 1723, the Cooper, with fix Hands in the Long-Boat, were going a-fhore at the Watering-place to fill their Casks; as he came along by the Schooner I called to him, and asked him if he were going afhore, he told me, *Yes;* then I asked him, if he would take me along with him; he feemed to hefitate at firft but I urged that I had never been on fhore yet, fince I firft came on board and I thought it very hard that I fhould be fo clofely confined, when every one elfe had the Liberty of going afhore, feveral Times, as there was Occafion. At length he took me in, imagining, I fuppofe, that there would be no Danger of my Running away in fo defolate uninhabited a Place as that was.

I went into the Boat with only *Ozenbrigs* Frock and Troufers on, and a mill'd Cap upon my Head, having neither Shirt, Shoes nor Stockings, nor any thing elfe about me; whereas, had I been aware of fuch an Opportunity but one quarter of an Hour before, could have provided my felf fomething better

better. However, thought I, if I can but once get footing on *Terra Firma,* tho' in never so bad Circumstances, I shall count it an happy Deliverance; for I was resolved, come what would, never to come on board again

Low had often told me (upon my asking him to send me away in some of the Vessels, which he dismissed after he had taken them) that I should go home when he did, and not before, and swore that I should never set foot on Shore till he did. But the Time for Deliverance was now come. G O D had order'd it that *Low* and *Spriggs,* and almost all the commanding Officers, were ashore upon an Island distinct from *Roatan,* where the Watering-place was; He presented me in sight, when the Long-Boat came by; (the only Opportunity I could have had) He had moved the Cooper to take me into the Boat, and under such Circumstances as render'd me least liable to Suspicion; and so I got ashore.

When we came first to Land, I was very active in helping to get the Casks out of the Boat, and rowling them up to the Watering-place; then I lay down at the Fountain, and took a hearty Draught of the cool Water; and anon,

I gradually ftrol'd along the Beech, picking up Stones and Shells, and looking about me; when I had got about Musket Shot off from them (tho' they had taken no Arms along with them in the Boat) I began to make up to the Edge of the Woods; when the Cooper fpying me, call'd after me, and asked me where I was going; I told him I was going to get fome Coco-Nuts, for there were fome Coco-Nut Trees juft before me. So foon as I had recovered the Woods, and loft fight of them, I betook my felf to my Heels, and ran as faft as the Thicknefs of the Bufhes and my naked Feet would let me. I bent my Courfe, not directly from them, but rather up behind them, which I continued till I had got a confiderable Way into the Woods, and yet not fo far from them but that I could hear their Talk when they faid any thing loud; and here I lay clofe in a great Thicket, being well affured, if they fhould take the Pains to hunt after me never fo carefully, they would not be able to find me.

After they had filled their Casks, and were about to go off, the Cooper called after me to come away; but I lay fnug in my Thicket, and would give him no

Anfwer,

Answer, tho' I plainly enough heard him. At length they set a hallooing for me, but I was still silent: I could hear them say to one another, *The D-g is lost in the Woods, and can't find the Way out again*, then they hallooed again, and cried, *he is run away, and won't come again*: The Cooper said, if he had thought I would have serv'd him so, he would not have brought me ashore. They plainly saw it would be in vain to seek for me in such hideous Woods and thick Bushes. When they were weary with hallooing, the Cooper at last, to shew his Good-will to me, (I can't but love and thank him for his Kindness) call'd out, *If you don't come away presently, I'll go off and leave you alone.* But all they could say was no Temptation to me to discover my self, and least of all, that of their going away and leaving me; for this was the very thing I desired, that I might be rid of them, and all that belong'd to them. So finding it in vain for them to wait any longer, they put off with their Water without me, and thus was I left upon a desolate Island destitute of all Help, and much out of the Way of all Travellers; however, I look'd upon this Wilderness as hospitable, and this Loneliness as
good

good Company , compared with the
State and Society I was now happily
delivered from.

When I supposed they were gone off,
I came out of my Thicket, and drew
down to the Water-side, about a Mile
below the Watering-place, where there
was a small Run of Water; and here
I sat down to observe their Motions, and
know when the Coast was clear; for I
could not but have some remaining Fears
left they should send a Company of Ar-
men Men after me, yet I thought if
they should, the Woods and Bushes
were so thick that it would be impossible
they should find me. As yet I had no
thing to eat, nor indeed were my
Thoughts much concerned about living
in this desolate Place, but they were
chiefly taken up about my getting clear.
And to my Joy, after the Vessels had
staid five Days in this Harbour, they
came to Sail, and put out to Sea, and
I plainly saw the Schooner part from
the two Sloops, and shape a different
Course from them.

When they were gone and the Coast
clear, I began to reflect upon my self,
and my present Condition; I was upon
an Island, from whence I could not get
off; I knew of no human Creature
within

within many fcores of Miles of me; I had but a fcanty Cloathing, and no Poffibility of getting more; I was deftitute of all Provifion for my Support, and knew not how I fhould come at any; every thing look'd with a difmal Face; the fad Profpect drew Tears from me in abundance; yet fince **GOD** had gracioufly granted my Defires, in freeing me out of the Hands of the Sons of Violence, whofe Bufinefs 'tis to devife Mifchief againft their Neighbour, and from whom every thing that had the leaft Face of Religion and Virtue was entirely banifh'd, (unlefs that *Low* would never fuffer his Men to work upon the Sabbath, (it was more devoted to play) and I have feen fome of them fit down to read in a good Book) therefore I purpofed to account all the Hardfhip I might now meet with, as light and eafy, compared with being affociated with them.

In order to find in what Manner I was to live for the Time to come, I began to range the Ifland over, which I fuppofe is about 10 or 11 Leagues long, in the Latitude of 16 deg. 30 min or thereabouts. I foon found that I muft look for no Company, but the wild Beaft of the Field, and the Fowl of the Air;

Air; with all of which I made a firm
Peace, and GOD said, *Amen*, to it. I
could difcover no Footfteps of any Habitation upon the Ifland; yet there was
one Walk of Lime-trees near a Mile
long, and every now and then I found
fome broken Shreds of earthen Pots,
fcattered here and there upon the Place,
which fome fay are the Remains of
the *Indians* that formerly lived upon the
Ifland.

This Ifland is well watered, and is
full of Hills, high Mountains, and low-
ly Vallies. The Mountains are covered over with a fort of fhrubby black
Pine, and are almoft inacceffible. The
Vallies abound with Fruit-Trees, and
are fo prodigioufly thick with an Un-
derbrufh, that 'tis difficult paffing.

The Fruit were Coco-Nuts; but
thefe I could have no Advantage from,
becaufe I had no Way of coming at the
Infide. There are Wild Figs and Vines
in abundance; thefe I chiefly lived upon, efpecially at firft. There is alfo a
fort of Fruit growing upon Trees fomewhat larger than an Orange, of an
oval Shape, of a brownifh Colour without and red within, having two or
three Stones about as large as a Wal-
nut in the midft: Tho' I faw many of
thefe

these fallen under the Trees, yet I dared not to meddle with them for some time, till I saw some Wild Hogs eat them with Safety, and then I thought I might venture upon them too after such Tasters, and I found them to be a very delicious sort of Fruit; they are called *Mammees Supporters*, as I learned afterwards. There are also a sort of small Beech-Plumb growing upon low Shrubs, and a larger sort of Plumb growing upon Trees, which are called Hog-Plumbs; and many other sorts of Fruit, which I am wholly a Stranger to. Only I would take notice of the Goodness of God to me, in preserving me from destroying my self by feeding upon any noxious Fruit, as the *Mangeneil* Apple, which I often took up in my Hands, and look'd upon, but had not the Power to eat of, which, if I had, it would have been present Death to me, as I was informed afterwards, tho' I knew not what it was.

There are also upon this Island, and the adjacent Islands and Keys, Deer and Wild Hogs. They abound too with Fowl of diverse sorts, as Ducks, Teal, Curlews, Galdings (a Fowl long-legged, and shaped somewhat like an Heron, but not so big,) Pelicans, Boobys,

Boobys, Pigeons, Parrots, &c. and the Shoars abound with Tortoise.

But of all this Store of Beast and Fowl, I could make no Use to supply my Necessities; tho' my Mouth often watered for a Bit of them, yet I was forced to go without it; for I had no Knife or other Instrument of Iron with me, by which to cut up a Tortoise when I had turned it, or to make Snares or Pits with which to entrap, or Bows and Arrows with which to kill any Bird or Beast withal; nor could I by any possible means that I knew of, come at Fire to dress any if I had taken them; tho' I doubt not but some would have gone down raw, if I could have come at it.

I sometimes had Thoughts of digging Pits and covering them over with small Branches of Trees, and laying Brush and Leaves upon them to take some Hogs or Deer in; but all was vain Imagination, I had no Shovel, neither could I find or make any thing that would answer my End, and I was presently convinced, that my Hands alone were not sufficient to make one deep and large enough to detain any thing that should fall into it, so that I was forc'd to rest satisfy'd with the Fruit of the Vine and Trees, and look'd upon it

I   as

as good Provision, and very handy for one in my Condition.

In Length of Time, as I was poking about the Beech with a Stick, to see if I could find any Tortoise Nests, (which I had heard lay their Eggs in the Sand) I brought up part of an Egg clinging to the Stick, and upon removing the Sand, which lay over them, I found near an hundred and fifty Eggs, which had not been laid long enough to spoil; so I took some of them and eat them: And in this Way I sometimes got some Eggs to eat, which I sometimes strung upon a Strip of Palmeto, and hung up in the Sun, where, in a few Days, they, would become thicken'd, and somewhat hard, as if they had been boiled, and so be more palatable; but after all, they are not very good at the best; yet what is not good to him that has nothing to live upon but what falls from the Trees?

The Tortoise lay their Eggs above High Water Mark, in a Hole which they make in the Sand, about a Foot, or a Foot and a half deep, and cover them over with the Sand, which they make as smooth and even as any part of the Beech, so that there is no discerning

E

cerning where they are, by any, the least Sign of a Hillock or Rifing; and according to my beft Obfervation, they hatch in about 18 or 20 Days, and as foon as the young ones are hatch'd they betake themfelves immediately to the Water.

There are many Serpents upon this and the adjacent Iflands. There is one fort that is very large, as big round as a Man's Wafte, tho' not above 12 or 14 Feet long. Thefe are called *Owlers.* They look like old fallen Stocks of Trees covered over with a fhort Mofs, when they lie at their Length; but they more ufually lie coiled up in a Round. The firft I faw of thefe greatly furprized me, for I was very near to it before I difcover'd it to be a living Creature, and then it open'd its Mouth wide enough to have thrown a Hat into it, and blew out its Breath at me. This Serpent is very flow in its Motion and nothing venomous; as I was afterwards told by a Man, who faid he had been once bitten by one of them. There are feveral other fmaller Serpents, fome of them very venomous, particularly one that is called a *Barber's Pole*, being ftreaked white and yellow. But I met wit with no Rattle-Snakes there, unleſs the Pirates, nor did I ever hear of any other being there.

The Iſlands are alſo greatly infeſted with vexatious Inſects, eſpecially the Musketto, and a ſort of ſmall black Fly; ſomething like a Gnat, more trouble-ſome than the Musketto; ſo that if one had never ſo many of the Comforts of Life about him, theſe Inſects would render his Living here very burthen-ſome to him, unleſs he retired to a ſmall Key, deſtitute of Woods and Bruſh, where the Wind diſperſes the Vermin.

The Sea hereabouts hath a Variety of Fiſh; ſuch as are good to eat I could not come at; and the Sharks, and Alligators, or Crocodiles, I did not care to have any thing to do with; tho' I was once greatly endanger'd by a Shark, as I ſhall tell afterwards.

This was the Place I was confined to, this my Society and Fellowſhip, and this my State and Condition of Life. Here I ſpent near nine Months, with-out Converſe with any living Creature; for the Parrots here had not been taught to ſpeak: Here I linger'd out one Day after another, I knew not how, without Buſineſs or Diverſion, unleſs gathering up my Food, rambling from

Hill

Hill to Hill, from Ifland to Ifland, ga-
zing upon the Water, and ftaring upon
the Face of the Sky, may be called
fo.

In this lonely and diftreffed Condition I had time to call over my paft
Life, and young as I was, I faw I had
grown old in Sin, my Tranfgreffions
were more than my Days; and though
GOD had gracioufly reftrained me
from the groffer Enormities of Life, yet
I faw Guilt ftaring me in the Face,
enough to humble me, and for ever to
vindicate the Juftice of GOD in all
that I underwent. I called to mind
many things I had heard from the
Pulpit, and what I had formerly read
in the Bible, which I was now wholly
deftitute of, tho' I thought if I could
but have one now, it would have fweet-
ned my Condition, by the very Di-
verfion of Reading; and much more
from the Direction and Comfort it
would have afforded me. I had fome
Comforts in the midft of my Calamity.
It was no fmall Support to me that I
was about my lawful Employment when
I was firft taken, and that I had no
Hand in bringing my Mifery upon my-
felf, but was forced away forely againft
my Will. It wonderfully alleviated my

Sorrows,

Sorrows, to think that I had my Parents Approbation and Confent in my going to Sea ; and I often fancied to my felf, that if I had gone to Sea againft their Will and Pleafure, and had met with this Difafter, I fhould have look'd upon it as a defign'd Punifhment of fuch Difobedience, and the very Reflection on it would have fo aggravated my Mifery, as foon to have put an end to my Days. I look'd upon my felf alfo, as more in the Way of the Divine Blefling now, than when I was link'd to a Crew of Pirates, where I could fcarce hope for Protection and a Blefling. I plainly faw very fignal Inftances of the Power and Goodnefs of G O D to me, in the many Deliverances which I had already experienc'd, (the leaft of which I was utterly unworthy of) and this encouraged me to put my Truft in Him ; and tho' I had none but GOD to go to for Help, yet I knew that he was able to do more for me than I could ask or think ; to Him therefore I committed my felf, purpofing to wait hopefully upon the LORD till He fhould fend Deliverance to me : Trufting that in His own Time and Way, He would find out Means for my fafe Return to my Father's Houfe ; and earneftly entreat-

ing

ing that He would provide a better Place for me.

It was my daily Practice to ramble from one Part of the Island to another, tho' I had a more special Home near to the Water-side. Here I had built me a House to defend me from the Heat of the Sun by Day, and the great Dews of the Night. I took some of the best Branches I could find fallen from the Trees, and stuck them in the Ground; and I contrived as often as I could (for I built many such Huts) to fix them leaning against the Limb of a Tree that hung low; I split the Palmeto Leaves and knotted the Limbs and Sticks together; then I covered them over with the largest and best Palmeto Leaves I could find. I generally situated my Hut near the Water-side, with the open Part of it facing the Sea, that I might be the more ready upon the Look-out, and have the Advantage of the Sea Breeze, which both the Heat and the Vermin required. But the Vermin (the Muskettos and Flies) grew so troublesome to me, that I was put upon Contrivance to get rid of their Company. This led me to think of getting over to some of the adjacent Keys, that I might have some Rest from the

the Diſturbance of theſe buſy Companions. My greateſt Difficulty lay in
getting over to any other Iſland, for I
was but a very poor Swimmer, and I
had no Canoe, nor any Means of making one. At length I got a Piece of
Bamboe, which is hollow like a Reed,
and light as a Cork, and having made
Trial of it under my Breaſt and Arms
in ſwimming by the Shoar, with this
Help I e'en ventur'd to put off for a
ſmall Key, about Gun-ſhot off, and I
reach'd it pretty comfortably. This
Key was but about 3 or 400 Feet in
Compaſs, clear of Woods and Bruſh,
and lay very low; and I found it ſo
free from the Vermin, by the free Paſ-
ſage of the Wind over it, that I ſeemed
to be got into a New World, where I
lived more at eaſe. This I kept as a
Place of Retreat, whither I retired
when the Heat of the Day rendered the Fly-kind moſt troubleſome to
me; for I was obliged to be much upon
Roatan for the Sake of my Food, Water and Houſe. When I ſwam backward and forward from my Night to
my Day-Iſland, I uſed to bind my Frock
and Trouſers about my Head, but I
could not ſo eaſily carry over Wood
and Leaves to make a Hut of, elſe I
ſhould

should have spent more of my Time upon my little Day-Island.

My swimming thus backward and forward exposed me to some Danger. Once, I remember, as I was passing from my Day to my Night-Island, the Bamboe got from under me e're I was aware, and the Tide or Current set so strong, that I was very difficultly put to it to recover the Shore; so that a few Rods more Distance had in all Probability landed me in another World. At another Time, as I was swimming over to my Day - Island, a shovel-nos'd Shark (of which the Seas thereabouts are full, as well as Alligators) struck me in the Thigh, just as I set my Foot to Ground, and so grounded himself (I suppose) by the Shoalness of the Water, that he could not turn himself to come at me with his Mouth, and so, through the Goodness of GOD, I escaped falling a Prey to his devouring Teeth. I felt the Blow he gave me some Hours after I had got ashore. By accustoming my self to swim, I at length grew pretty dexterous at it, and often gave my self the Diversion of thus passing from one Island to another among the Keys.

One of my greatest Difficulties lay in my being bare-foot; my Travels backward

ward and forward in the Woods to hunt
for my daily Food, among the thick Un-
derbrush, where the Ground was covered
with sharp Sticks and Stones, and upon
the hot Beech, among the sharp broken
Shells, had made so many Wounds and
Gashes in my Feet, and some of them
very large, that I was hardly able to
go at all. Very often as I was treading
with all the Tenderness I could, a sharp
Stone or Shell on the Beech, or point-
ed Stick in the Woods, would run into
the old Wounds, and the Anguish of it
would strike me down as suddenly as if
I had been shot thro', and oblige me
to set down and weep, by the Hour
together, at the Extremity of my Pain ;
so that in Process of Time I could
travel no more than needs must, for the
necessary procuring of Food. Sometimes I have sat leaning my Back against
a Tree, with my Face to the Sea, to
look out for the passing of a Vessel, for
a whole Day together.

At length I grew very weak and
faint, as well as sore and bruised ; and
once while I was in this Condition, a
wild Boar seem'd to make at me with
some Fierceness ; I knew not what to
do with my self, for I was not able to
defend my self against him if he should

attack

attack me. So as he drew nearer to me, I caught hold of the Limb of a Tree, which was close by me, and drew my Body up by it from the Ground, as well as I could; while I was in this hanging Posture, the Boar came and struck at me, but his Tushes only took hold on my shattered Trousers, and tore a Piece out; and then he went his Way. This, I think, was the only Time that I was assaulted by any wild Beast, with whom I said I had made Peace; and I look upon it as a great Deliverance.

As my Weakness increased upon me, I should often fall down as though struck with a dead Sleep, and many a time as I was thus falling, and sometimes when I laid my self down to sleep, I never expected to wake or rise more; and yet in the midst of all GOD has wonderfully preserv'd me.

In the midst of this my great Soreness and Feebleness I lost the Days of the Week; and how long I had lain in some of my benumb'd sleepy Fits, I knew not, so that I was not able now to distinguish the Sabbath from any other Day of the Week; tho' all Days were in some sort a Sabbath to me. As my Illness prevailed, I wholly lost the Month,

Month, and knew not whereabouts I was in the Account of Time.

Under all this dreadful Diftrefs, I had no healing Balfams to apply to my Feet, no Cordials to revive my fainting Spirits, hardly able now and then to get me fome Figs or Grapes to eat, nor any poffible way of coming at a Fire, which the cool Winds and great Rains beginning to come on, now called for. The Rains begin about the middle of *October*, and continue for five Months together, and then the Air is raw and cold, like our North-eaft Storms of Rain, only at times the Sun breaks out with fuch an exceeding Fiercenefs, that there is hardly any enduring the Heat of it.

I had often heard of the fetching Fire by rubbing of two Sticks together, but I could never get any this Way, tho' I had often tried while I was in Health and Strength, until I was quite tir'd. Afterwards I learned the Way of getting Fire from two Sticks, which I will publifh, that it may be of Service to any that may be hereafter in my Condition.

Take two Sticks, the one of harder, the other of fofter Wood, the dryer the better; in the foft Wood make a fort of Mortice or Socket, point the harder Wood to fit that Socket, hold the softer Wood firm between the Knees, take the harder Wood between your Hands with the Point fix'd in the Socket, and rub the Stick in your Hands backward and forward briskly, like a Drill, and it will take Fire in less than a Minute, as I have sometimes since seen, upon Experiment made of it.

But then I knew of no such Method, (and it may be should have been difficultly put to it to have formed the Mortice and Drill for want of a Knife) and I suffer'd greatly without a Fire, through the Chillness of the Air, the Wetness of the Season, and living only upon raw Fruit.

Thus I pass'd about nine Months in this lonely, melancholy, wounded and languishing Condition. I often laid my self down as upon my last Bed, and concluded I should certainly die alone, and no Body know what was become of me. I thought it would be some Relief to me if my Parents could but tell where I was; and then I thought their Distress would be exceeding great, if they knew what I underwent. But all such Thoughts were vain. The more my Difficulties increased, and the

nearer

nearer Profpect I had of Dying, the more it drove me upon my Knees, and made me the more earneft in my Cries to my Maker for His favourable Regards to me, and to the Great Redeemer to pardon me, and provide for my after Well-being.

And fee the furprifing Goodnefs of GOD to me, in fending me Help in my Time of Trouble, and that in the moft unexpected Way and Manner, as tho' an Angel had been commiffioned from Heaven to relieve me.

Sometime in *November*, 1723, I efpied a fmall Canoe, coming towards me, with one Man in it. It did not much furprize me. A Friend I could not hope for; and I could not refift, or hardly get out of the Way of an Enemy; nor need I fear one. I kept my Seat upon the Edge of the Beech. As he came nearer he difcover'd me, and feem'd greatly furpriz'd. He called to me. I told him whence I was, and that he might fafely venture afhore, for I was alone, and almoft dead As e came up to me, he ftar'd and look'd old with Surprize; my Garb and ountenance aftonifh'd him; he knew t what to make of me; he ftarted ack a little, and view'd me more thoughly; but upon recovering of him-

F   felf,

felf, he came forward, and took me by the Hand, and told me he was glad to fee me. And he was ready, as long as he ftaid with me, to do any kind Offices for me.

He proved to be a *North-Britain,* a Man well in Years, of a grave and venerable Afpect, and of a referved Temper. His Name I never knew, for I had not ask'd him in the little Time he was with me, expecting a longer Converfe with him; and he never told me it. But he acquainted me that he had liv'd with the *Spaniards* 22 Years, and now they threaten'd to burn him; I knew not for what Crime: Therefore he had fled for Sanctuary to this Place and brought his Gun, Ammunition and Dog, with a fmall Quantity of Pork, defigning to fpend the Refidue of his Days here, and fupport himfelf b Hunting. He feem'd very kind an obliging to me, gave me fome of h Pork, and affifted me in all he could tho' he convers'd little.

Upon the third Day after he came me, he told me he would go out in his C noe among the Iflands, to kill fome w Hogs and Deer, and would have had to go along with him. His Compa the Fire, and a little drefs'd Provifi fomething recruited my Spirits; yet I was fo weak, and fore in my F that I could not accompany him in Hunting : So he set out alone; and said he would be with me again in a few Hours. The Sky was serene and fair, and there was no Prospect of any Danger in his little Voyage among the islands, when he had come safe in that small Float near 12 Leagues; but by that time he had been gone an Hour, there arose a most violent Gust of Wind and Rain, which in all Probability over-set him ; so that I never saw or heard of him any more. And though by this Means I was depriv'd of my Companion, yet it was the Goodness of GOD to me, that I was not well enough to go with him ; for thus I was preserved from that Destruction which undoubtedly overtook him.

Thus after the Pleasure of having a Companion almost three Days, I was as unexpectedly reduc'd to my former lonely Condition, as I had been for a little while recover'd out of it. It was grievous to me to think, that I no sooner saw the Dawnings of Light, after so long Obscurity, but the Clouds returned after the Rain upon me. I began to experience the Advantage of a Companion, and find that two is better than one, and flatter'd my self, that by the Help of

some-

some fresh Hogs Grease, I should get my Feet well, and by a better Living, recover more Strength. But it pleas'd GOD to take from me the only Man I had seen for so many Months, after so short a Converse with him. Yet I was left in better Circumstances by him than he found me in: For, at his going away, he left with me about five Pound of Pork, a Knife, a Bottle of Gun-Powder, Tobacco, Tongs, and Flint, by which means I was in a Way to live better than I had done. For now I could have a Fire, which was very needful for me, the rainy Months of the Winter; I could cut up some Tortoise when I had turned them, and have a delicate broil'd Meal of it: So that by the Help of the Fire, and dress'd Food, and the Blessing of GOD attending it, I began to recover more Strength, only my Feet remain'd fore.

Besides, I had this Advantage now, which I had not before, that I could go out now and then and catch a Dish of Cray-Fish, a Fish much like a Lobster, only wanting the great Claws. My manner of catching them was odd; I took some of the best Pieces of the old broken small Wood, that came the nearest to our Pitch-Pine, or Candle-Wood,

and

and made them up into a small Bundle like a Torch, and holding one of these lighted at one End in one Hand, I waded into the Water upon the Beech up to the Waste; the Cray-Fish spying the Light at a considerable Distance, would crawl away till they came directly under it, and then they would lie still at my Feet. In my other Hand I had a forked Stick, with which I struck the Fish and tossed it ashoar. In this manner I supply'd my self with a Mess of Shell-Fish, which when roasted is very good eating.

Between two and three Months after I had lost my Companion, as I was ranging a long Shoar, I found a small Canoo; The Sight of this at first renewed my Sorrows for his Loss; for I thought it had been his Canoo, and its coming a shoar thus, was a Proof to me that he was lost in the Tempest; but upon further Examination of it, I found it was one I had never seen before.

When I had got this little Vessel in Possession, I began to think my self Admiral of the neighbouring Seas, as well as sole Possessor and chief Commander upon the Islands; and with the Advantage hereof I could transport my self to my small Islands of Retreat, much more

conve-

conveniently than in my former Method of swimming. In Process of Time I thought of making a Tour to some of the more distant and larger Islands, to see after what manner they were inhabited, and how they were provided, and partly to give my self the Liberty of Diversions. So I laid in a small Parcel of Grapes and Figs, and some Tortoise, and took my Fire-works with me, and put off for the Island of *Bonacco*, an Island of about 4 or 5 Leagues long, and some 5 or 6 Leagues to the Eastward of *Roatan*.

As I was upon my Voyage, I discover'd a Sloop at the Eastern End of the Island; so I made the best of my way, and put in at the Western End, designing to travel down to them by Land, partly because there ran out a large Point of Rocks far into the Sea, and I did not care to venture my self so far out in my little Canoo, as I must do to head them; and partly because I was willing to make a better Discovery of them before I was seen by them; for in the midst of my most deplorable Circumstances I could never entertain the Thoughts of returning on board any Pirate, if I should have the Opportunity, but had rather live and die as I

was.

was. So I hall'd up my Canoo, and fa-
ftened her as well as I could, and fet
out upon my Travel.

I fpent two Days and the biggeft part
of two Nights in travelling of it. My
Feet were yet fo fore, that I could go
but very flowly; and fometimes the
Woods and Bufhes were fo thick, that
I was forced to crawl upon my Hands
and Knees for half a Mile together.
In this Travel I met with an odd Adventure, that had like to have proved
fatal to me, and my Prefervation was
an eminent Inftance of the Divine Conduct and Protection.

As I drew within a Mile or two of
where I fuppofed the Sloop might be,
I made down to the Water-fide, and
flowly opened the Sea, that I might not
difcover my felf too foon. When I came
down to the Water-fide, I could fee no
Sign of the Sloop, upon which I concluded that it was gone clear, while I
fpent fo much Time in Travelling. I
was very much tired with my long te-
dious March, and fat my felf down
leaning againft the Stock of a Tree facing the Sea, and fell afleep. But I
had not flept long, before I was awakened in a very furprizing manner by
the Noife of Guns. I ftarted up in a
Fright,

Fright, and saw nine Periaguas, or large Canooes, full of Men firing upon me. I soon turned about and ran, as fast as my sore Feet would let me, into the Bushes, and the Men, which were *Spaniards*, cried after me, *O English-man, we'll give you good Quarter.* But such was the Surprize I had taken, by being awakened out of Sleep in such a manner, that I had no Command of my self to hearken to their Offers of Quarter, which it may be at another time under cooler Thoughts I might have done. So I made into the Woods, and they continued firing after me to the Number of 150 small Shot at least, many of which cut off several small Twigs of the Bushes along-side of me as I went off. When I had got out of the Reach of their Shot into a very great Thicket, I lay close for several Hours; and perceiving they were gone, by the Noise of their Oars in rowing off, I came out of my Thicket, and travelled a Mile or two along the Water-side below the Place where they fired upon me, and then I saw the Sloop under *English* Colours sailing out of the Harbour, with the Periaguas in Tow; and then I concluded that it was an *English* Sloop that had been at the

Bay,

Bay, whom the *Spaniards* had met with and taken.

The next Day I went up to the Tree where I so narrowly escaped being taken napping, and there to my Surprize I found six or seven Shot had gone into the Body of the Tree, within a Foot or less of my Head, as I sat down ; and yet thro' the wonderful Goodness of God to me, in the midst of all their Fire, (and tho' I was as a Mark set up for them to shoot at) none of their Shot touched me. So did God as yet signally preserve me.

After this I travelled away for my Canoo, at the Western End of the Island, and spent near three Days e'er I reached it. In this long March backward and forward, I suffered very much from the Soreness of my Feet and the Want of Provision ; for this Island is not so plentifully stored with Fruit as *Roatan* is, so that I was very difficultly put to it for my Subsistence for the five or six Days that I spent here ; and besides the Musketos and Black Flies were abundantly more numerous and vexatious to me than at my old Habitation. The Difficulties I met with here made me lay aside all Thoughts of tarrying any Time to search the Island. At

length,

length, much tired and fpent, I reached my Canoo, and found all fafe there,
to my great Joy ; and then I put off for
Roatan, which was a Royal Palace to me;
in comparifon of *Bonacco,* where I ar-
rived, to my great Satisfaction, about
Ten o' Clock at Night, and found all
things as I left them.

Here I liv'd (if it may be call'd living) alone for about feven Months
more, from the Time of my lofing my
North-Britifh Companion, and fpent my
Time after my ufual Manner, in hunting for my Food, and ranging the I-
flands, till at length it pleas' GOD to
fend fome Company to me, with whom
I could converfe, and enjoy fomewhat
more of the Comforts of Life.

Sometime in *June,* 1724, as I was upon my fmall Ifland, where I often retir'd for Shelter from the peftering In-
fects, I faw two large Canoes making
into the Harbour ; as they drew near,
they faw the Smoke of the Fire which I
had kindled, and wondering what it
fhould mean, came to a Stand. I had
frefh in my Memory what I had met
with at *Bonacco,* and was very loth to
run the Rifque of fuch another Firing,
and therefore ftept to my Canoo, upon
the Backfide of my fmall Ifland, not
above

above 100 Feet off from me, and immediately went over to my great Mansion, where I had Places of Safety, to shelter me from the Designs of an Enemy, and Rooms large and spacious enough to give a kindly Welcome to any ordinary Number of Friends. They saw me cross the Ferry, of about Gun-shot over, from my little to my great Island, and being as much afraid of *Spaniards* as I was of Pirates, they drew very cautiously towards the Shore. I came down upon the Beech, shewing my self openly to them; for their Caution made me think they were no Pirates, and I did not much care who else they were; however, I thought I could call to them, and know what they were, before I should be in much Danger from their Shot; and if they proved such as I did not like, I could easily retire from them. But before I called, they, who were as full of Fears as I could be, lay upon their Oars, and hallooed to me, enquiring who I was, and whence I came; I told them I was an *Englishman,* and had run away from the Pirates. Upon this they drew something nearer, and enquired who was there besides my self; I assured them I was alone. Then I took my Turn, and asked them who

they

they were, and whence they came. They told me they were *Baymen*, come from the *Bay*. This was comfortable News to me; so I bid them pull ashore, there was no Danger; I would stop for them. Accordingly they put ashore, but at some Distance from me, and first sent one Man ashore to me; whom I went to meet. When the Man came up to me, he started back, frighted to see such a poor, ragged, lean, wan, forlorn wild, miserable Object so near him; but upon recovering himself, he came and took me by the Hand, and we fell to embracing one another; he with Surprize and Wonder, I with a sort of Extafy of Joy. After this was over, he took me up in his Arms, and carry'd me down to their Canoes, where they were all struck with Astonishment at the Sight of me, were glad to receive me, and express'd a very great Tenderness to me.

I gave them a short History how I had escaped from *Low*, and had liv'd here alone for sixteen Months, (saving three Days) what Hardship I had met with; and what Danger I had run thro'. They stood amaz'd! they wonder'd I was alive! and express'd a great Satisfaction in it, that they were come to re-

I   lieve

lieve me. And obferving I was weak, and my Spirits low, they gave me about a Spoonful of Rum to recruit my fainting Spirits. This fmall Quantity, (thro' my long difufe of any Liquor higher fpirited than Water) and my prefent Weaknefs, threw my animal Spirits into fuch a violent Agitation, as to obftruct their regular Motion, and produced a kind of Stupor, which left me for fome time bereft of all Senfe ; fome of them perceiving me falling into fuch a ftrange Infenfibility, would have given me more of the fame Spirit to have recover'd me ; but thofe of them that had more WIT, would not allow of it. So I lay for fome fmall time in a fort of a Fit, and they were ready to think that they fhould lofe me as foon as they had found me. But I revived.

And when I was fo thoroughly come to my felf as to converfe with them, I found they were eighteen Men come from the Bay of *Honduras,* the chief of which were, *John Hope,* and *John Ford.* The Occafion of their coming from the *Bay* was a Story they had got among them, that the *Spaniards* had projected to make a Defcent upon them by Water, while the *Indians* were to affault them by Land, and cut off the *Bay* ; and they

G   retir'd

retir'd hither to avoid the Destruction that was design'd. This *John Hope* and *John Ford* had formerly, upon a like Occasion, shelter'd themselves among these Islands, and liv'd for four Years together upon a small Island called *Barbarat*, about two Leagues from *Roatan*, where they had two Plantations, as they called them; and being now upon the same Design of retreating for a time for Safety, they brought with them two Barrels of Flower, with other Provisions, their Fire-Arms, Ammunition, and Dogs for Hunting, and Nets for Tortoise, and an *Indian* Woman to dress their Provision for them. They chose for their chief Residence a small Key about a quarter of a Mile round, lying near to *Barbarat*, which they call'd the *Castle of Comfort*, chiefly because it was low, and clear of Woods and Bushes, where the Wind had an open Passage, and drove away the pestering Musketos and Gnats. From hence they sent to the other Islands round about for Wood and Water, and for Materials with which they built two Houses, such as they were, for Shelter.

And now I seem'd to be in a far more likely Way to live pretty tollerably than in the sixteen Months past, for besides

besides the having Company, they treated me with a great deal of Civility, in their Way; they cloàth'd me, and gave me a large wrapping Gown to lodge in a-Nights, to defend me from the great Dews, till their Houses were cover'd; and we had Plenty of Provision But after all, they were bad Company, and there was but little Difference between them and the Pirates, as to their common Conversation, only I thought they were not now engaged in any such bad Design as render'd it unlawful to join with them, nor dangerous to be found in their Company.

In Process of time, by the Blessing of GOD, and the Assistance I received from them, I gather'd so much Strength, that I was able sometimes to go out a hunting with them. The Islands hereabouts, I observ'd before, abound with wild Hogs and Deer, and Tortoise. Their Manner was, to go out a Number of them in a Canoe, sometimes to one Island, sometimes to another, and kill what Game they could meet with, and juk their Pork, by beginning at one End of a Hog, and cutting along to the other End, and so back again till they had gone all over him, and flee the Flesh in long Strings off from the

G 2　　　　　Bones;

Bones; the Venifon they took whole, or in Quarters, and the Tortoife in like Manner; and return'd home with a Load of it; what they did not fpend prefently, they hung up in their Houfe a Smoak-drying; and this was a ready Supply to 'em at all Times.

I was now ready to think my felf out of the Reach of any Danger from an Enemy; for what fhould bring any here? and I was encompafs'd continually with a Number of Men, with their Aims ready at hand; and yet when I thought my felf moft fecure, I very narrowly efcaped falling again into the Hands of the Pirates.

It happen'd, about fix or feven Months after thefe *Baymen* came to me, that 3 Men and I took a Canoe, with 4 Oars, to go over to *Bonacco*, a hunting, and to kill Tortoife. While we were gone the reft of the *Baymen* haled up their Canoes, and dry'd and tarr'd them, in order to go to the *Bay*, and fee how Matters ftood there, and to fetch off their Effects which they had left behind them, in cafe they fhould find there was no Safety for them in tarrying. But before they were gone, we, who had met with good Succefs in our Voyage, were upon our Return to them, with

a

a full Load of Tortoise and jirkt Pork:
As we were upon entring into the
Mouth of the Harbour, in a Moon-light
Evening, we saw a great Flash of Light,
and heard the Report of a Gun, which
we thought was much louder than a
Musket, out of a large Periagua, which
we saw near our *Castle of Comfort.* This
put us into a great Consternation, and
we knew not what to make of it. Within a Minute or two, we heard a Volley
of 18 or 20 small Arms discharged upon
the Shoar, and heard some Guns also
fir'd off from the Shore. Upon which
we were satisfied, that some Enemy,
Pirates or *Spaniards,* were attacking our
People ; and being cut off from our
Companions by the Periaguas which
lay between us and them, we thought
it our wisest Way to save our selves as
well as we could : So we took down
our little Mast and Sail, that it might
not betray us, and rowed out of the
Harbour as fast as we could, thinking
to make our Escape from them undis-
cover'd, to an Island about a Mile and a
half off; but they either saw us before
we had taken our Sail down, or heard
the Noise of our Oars, as we made out
of the Harbour, and came after us with
all Speed, in a Periagua of eight or ten

Oars

Oars. We faw them coming, and that they gain'd Ground upon us apace, and therefore pull'd up for Life, refolving to reach the neareft Shore, if poffible. The Periagua overhaled us fo faft, that they difcharg'd a Swivel Gun at us, which over-fhot us; but we made a Shift to gain the Shore before they were come fairly within the Reach of their fmall Arms, which yet they fir'd upon us as we were getting afhore. Then they call'd to us, and told us they were Pirates, and not *Spaniards*, and we need not fear, they would give us good Quarter, fuppofing this would eafily move us to furrender our felves to them. But they could not have mention'd any thing worfe to difcourage me from having any thing to do with them, for I had the utmoft Dread of a Pirate; and my firft Averfion to them was now ftrengthned with the juft Fears, that if I fhould fall into their Hands again, they would foon make a Sacrifice of me for my deferting them. I therefore concluded to keep as clear of them as I could; and the *Baymen* with me had no great Inclination to be medling with them, and fo we made the beft of our Way into the Woods. They took away our Canoe from us, and all that

that was in it, refolving, if we would not come to them, they would ftrip us as far as they were able, of all Means of Subfiftance where we were. I, who had known what it was to be deftitute of all things, and alone, was not much concern'd about that, now that I had Company, and they their Arms with them, fo that we could have a Supply of Provifion by Hunting, and Fire to drefs it with.

This Company it feems were fome of *Spriggs* Men, who was Commander of the Schooner when I ran away from them. This fame *Spriggs,* I know not upon what Occafion, had caft off the Service of *Low,* and fet up for himfelf as the Head of a Party of Rovers, and had now a good Ship of 24 Guns, and a *Barmuda* Sloop of 12 Guns, under his Command, which were now lying in *Roatan* Harbour, where he put in to water and clean, at the Place where I firft made my Efcape. He had difcover'd our People upon the fmall Ifland, where they refided, and fent a Periagua full of Men to take them. Accordingly they took all the Men afhore, and with them an *Indian* Woman and Child; thofe of them that were afhore abufed the Woman fhamefully. They kill'd
one

one Man after they were come afhore, and threw him into one of the *Baymens* Canoes where their Tar was, and fet Fire to it, and burnt him in it. Then they carry'd our People on board their Veffels, where they were barbaroufly treated.

One of the *Baymen*, *Thomas Grande*, turn'd Pirate; and he being acquainted that old Father *Hope* (as we call'd him) had hid many things in the Woods, told the Pirates of it, who beat poor *Hope* unmercifully, and made him go and fhew them where he had hid his Treafure, which they took away from him.

After they had kept the *Baymen* on board their Veffels for five Days, then they gave them a Flat of about five or fix Tons to carry them to the *Bay* in, but they gave them no Provifion for their Voyage; and before they fent them away, they made them fwear to 'em not to come near us, who had made our Efcape upon another Ifland. All the while the Veffels rode in the Harbour, we kept a good Look-out, but were put to fome Difficulties, becaufe we did not dare to make a Fire to drefs our Victuals by, leaft it fhould difcover whereabouts we were, fo, that we were forc'd to live upon raw Provifion for
five

five Days. But as foon as they were gone, Father *Hope*, with his Company of *Baymen*, (little regarding an Oath that was forc'd from them; and thinking it a wicked Oath, better broken, than to leave four of us in fuch a helplefs Condition) came to us, and acquainted us who they were, and what they had done.

Thus the watchful Providence of GOD, which had fo often heretofore appeared on my Behalf, again took fpecial Care of me, and fent me out of the way of Danger. 'Tis very apparent, that if I had been with my Companions, at the ufual Place of Refidence, I had been taken with them,; and if I had, it is beyond queftion (humanly fpeaking) that I fhould not have efcaped with Life, if I fhould the moft painful and cruel Death, that the Madnefs and Rage of *Spriggs* could have invented for me; who would now have called to mind the Defign I was ingag'd in while we were parted from *Low*, as well as my final deferting of them. But, bleffed be GOD, who had Defigns of Favour for me, and fo order'd that I muft at this time be abfent from my Company.

Now

Now old Father *Hope* and his Company are all defigned for the *Bay*; only one *John Symonds*, who had a Negro belonging to him, purpofed to tarry here for fome Time, and carry on fome fort of Trade with the *Jamaica* Men upon the Main. I long'd to get home to *New-England*, and thought if I went to the *Bay* with them, it was very probable that I fhould in a little while meet with fome *New-England* Veffel, that would carry me to my native Country, from which I had been fo long a poor Exile. I ask'd Father *Hope*, if he would take me in with him, and carry me to the *Bay*. The old Man, though he feem'd glad of my Company, yet told me the many Difficulties that lay in the way; as that their Flat was but a poor thing to carry fo many Men in for near 70 Leagues, which they muft go before they would be out of the Reach of Danger; that they had no Provifion with them, and it was uncertain how the Weather would prove; they might be a great while upon their Paffage thither, and their Flat could very poorly endure a great Sea; that when they fhould come to the *Bay*, they knew not how they fhould meet with things there, and they were daily in

Danger

Danger of being cut off; and it may be, I should be longer there, in cafe all was well, than I car'd for, e'er I should meet with a Paffage for *New-England;* for the *New-England* Veffels often fail'd from the *Bay* to other Ports; fo that all things confider'd, he thought I had better ftay where I was, feeing I was like to have Company, whereas rather than I fhould be left alone, he would take me in.

On the other hand, *Symonds,* who, as I faid, defign'd to fpend fome time here, greatly urg'd me to ftay and bear him company. He told me, that as foon as the Seafon would permit, he purpofed to go over to the Main to the *Jamaica* Traders, where I might get a Paffage to *Jamaica,* and from thence to *New-England,* probably quicker, and undoubtedly much fafer than I could from the *Bay;* and that in the mean while I fhould fare as he did.

I did not trouble my felf much about Faring, for I knew I could not fare harder than I had done, but I thought, upon the Confideration of the whole, that there feem'd to be a fairer Profpect of my getting home by the way of *Jamaica,* than the *Bay;* and therefore I faid no more to Father *Hope* about going

with

with him, but concluded to stay. So I thank'd Father *Hope* and Company for all their Civilities to me, wishing them a good Voyage, and took leave of them.

And now there was *John Symonds*, and I, and his Negro, left behind; and a good Providence of GOD was it for me, that I took their Advice, and staid; for tho' I got not home by the way of *Jamaica*, as was proposed, yet I did another and quicker Way, in which there was more evident Interpositions of the Conduct of Divine Providence, as you will hear presently.

Symonds was provided with a Canoe, Fire-Arms, and two Dogs, as well as a Negro; with these he doubted not but we should be furnish'd with all that was necessary for our Subsistence. With this Company I spent between two and three Months, after the usual Manner, in hunting and ranging the Islands. And yet the Winter Rains would not suffer us to hunt much more than needs must.

When the Season was near approaching for the *Jamaica* Traders to be over at the Main, *Symonds* proposed the going to some of the other Islands that abounded more with Tortoise, that he might get the Shells of them, and carry to the Traders, and in Exchange furnish him-

himself with Ozenbrigs and Shoes, and such other Necessaries as he wanted. We did so, and having got good Store of Tortoise-Shell, he then proposed to go first for *Bonacco,* which lies nearer to the Main than *Roatan,* that from thence we might take a favourable Snatch to run over.

Accordingly we went to *Bonacco,* and by that time we had been there about five Days, there arose a very hard North Wind, which blew exceeding fierce, and lasted for about three Days; when the Heaft of the Storm was over, we saw several Vessels standing in for the Harbour; their Number and Largeness made me hope they might be Friends, and now an Opportunity was coming in which Deliverance might be perfected to me.

The larger Vessels came to Anchor at a great Distance off; but a Brigantine came over the Shoals, nearer in against the Watering-place, (for *Bonacco* as well as *Roatan* abounds with Water) which sent in her Boat with Casks for Water: I plainly saw they were *Englishmen,* and by their Garb and Air, and Number, being but three Men in the Boat, concluded they were Friends, and shew'd my self openly upon the

H Beech

Beech before them; as foon as they
faw me, they ftop'd rowing, and call'd
out to me to know who I was; I told
'em; and enquir'd who they were. They
let me know they were honeft Men, a-
bout their lawful Bufinefs. I then called to them to come afhore, for there
was no body here that would hurt them.
They came afhore, and a happy Meeting it was for me. Upon Enquiry, I
found that the Veffels were the *Dia-
mond* Man of War, and a Fleet under
his Convoy, bound to *Jamaica*, (many
whereof fhe had parted with in the late
Storm) which by the Violence thereof
had been forc'd fo far fouthward; and
the Man of War wanting Water, by
reafon of the Sicknefs of her Men, which
occafion'd a great Confumption of it,
had touch'd here, and fent in the Brigantine to fetch off Water for her. Mr.
Symonds, who at firft kept at the other
end of the Beech, about half a Mile off,
(left the three Men in the Boat fhould
refufe to come afhore, feeing two of us
together) at length came up to us, and
became a Sharer in my Joy, and yet
not without fome very confiderable Re-
luctance at the Thoughts of parting.
The Brigantine proved to be of *Salem*,
(within two or three Miles of my Father's

ther's Houfe) Capt. *Dove* Commander, a Gentleman whom I knew. So now I had the Profpect of a direct Paffage home. I fent off to Capt. *Dove*, to know if he would give me a Paffage home with him, and he was very ready to comply with my Defire ; and upon my going on board' him, befides the great Civilities he treated me with, he took me into pay ; for he had loft a Hand, and needed me to fupply his Place. The next Day the Man of War fent her Long-Boat in, full of Casks, which they fill'd with Wa-er, and put on board the Brigantine, who carry'd them off to her. I had one Difficulty more to encounter with, which was to take Leave of Mr. *Symonds*, who wept heartily at parting ; but this I was forc'd to go thro' for the Joy of getting Home.

So the latter end of *March*, 1725, we came to fail, and kept Company with the Man of War, who was bound to *Jamaica* . The firft of *April* we parted, and thro' the good Hand of GOD upon us, came fafe thro' the Gulf of *Florida*, to *Salem* Harbour, where we arriv'd upon *Saturday* Evening, the firft of *May* ; two Years, ten Months and fifteen Days, after I was firft taken by the Pirate *Low*, and two Years, and near two

Months after I had made my Escape,
from him upon *Roatan* Island. I went
the same Evening to my Father's House,
where I was receiv'd, as one coming to
them from the Dead, with all imaginable Surprize of Joy.

Thus I have given you a short Account, how God has conducted me thro'
a great Variety of Hardships and Dangers, and in all appear'd wonderfully
gracious to me. And I cannot but take
Notice of the strange Concurrence of
Divine Providence all along, in saving
me from the Rage of the Pirates, and
the Malice of the *Spaniards*, from the
Beasts of the Field, and the Monsters
of the Sea; in keeping me alive amidst
so many Deaths, in such a lonely and
helpless Condition; and in bringing a-
bout my Deliverance; the last Articles
whereof are as peculiarly remarkable as
any; — I must be just then gone over to
Bonacco; — a Storm must drive a Fleet
of Ships so far southward; — and their
Want of Water must oblige them to put
in at the Island where I was; — and a
Vessel bound to my own Home must
come and take me in. — *Not unto Men
and Means, but unto thy Name, O Lord, be
all the Glory!* Amen.

PHILIP ASHTON, *Jun.*

A SHORT

ACCOUNT

OF

Mr. *Nicholas Merritt's*

ESCAPE from the PIRATES, and his Sufferings till his Return Home.

 WAS taken by the Pirate *Low*, in at Port *Roſſaway*, at the ſame Time my Kinſman *Philip Aſhton* was; and while I continu'd under *Low's* Cuſtody, was us'd much as he was; and all my Intreaties of him to free me were but in vain, as you have ſeen ſomething of in the foregoing Hiſtory :

H 3   So

So that I shall not inlarge in telling how it far'd with me under the Pirates Hands, but only give some short Account of the Manner of my Escape from them, and what I met with afterwards, till I arriv'd at *Marble-Head*, where I belong.

Low had with him the *Rose* Pink, the Schooner, and a Sloop taken from one *Pier* of *Bristol*, and was standing away for *Bonavista*. I, who was on board the Schooner, had been greatly abused by an old Pirate, whom they call'd *Jacob*, but what his Sirname was, I know not: I desir'd some that were upon occasion going on board *Low*, to acquaint him how much I was beat and abus'd by old *Jacob*; they did so; and *Low* order'd me to be put on board the Sloop. Thus the Foundation of my Escape was laid, and my Sufferings proved the Means of my Deliverance.

On board the Sloop there were nine Hands, (one of them a *Portugueze*) whom *Low* had no Suspicion of, but thought he could trust them as much as any Men he had; and when I came on board, I made the Tenth Man. We perceiv'd that the Sloop greatly wrong'd both the Pink and Schooner; and there were six of us (as we found by sounding one another

another at a Diftance) that wanted to get away. When we underftood one another's Minds pretty fully, we refolved upon an Efcape. Accordingly, the fifth of *September*, 1722, a little after Break of Day, all Hands being upon Deck, three of us fix went forward, and three aft, and one *John Rhodes*, who was a ftout Hand, ftep'd into the Cabin, and took a couple of Piftols in his Hands, and ftood at the Cabin Door, and faid, If there were any that would go along with him, they fhould be welcome, for he defign'd to carry the Sloop home, and furrender himfelf; but if any Man attempted to make Refiftance, he fwore he would fhoot down the firft Man that ftirr'd. There being five of us that wanted to gain our Liberty, he was fure of us, and as for the other four, they faw plainly it was in vain for them to attempt to oppofe us. So we haled clofe upon a Wind, and ftood away.

When we parted with *Low*, we had but a very little Water aboard, and but two or three Pieces of Meat among us all; but we had Bread enough. We defign'd for *England*, but our Want of Water was fo great, being put to half a Pint a Man, for a Day, and that very muddy,

muddy and foul, from the Time we parted with *Low*, and meeting with no Veſſel of whom we could beg a Supply, that it made us come to a Reſolution to put in at the firſt Port; ſo we ſteer'd for *St Michaels*, where we arriv'd *September* 26.

So ſoon as we got in, we ſent a Man or two aſhore, to inform who we were, and to get us ſome Proviſions and Water. The Conſul, who was a *French* Proteſtant, with a Magiſtrate, and ſome other Officers, came on board us, to whom we gave an Account of our ſelves, and our Circumſtances. The Conſul told us, there ſhould not a Hair of our Heads be hurt. Upon which we were all carry'd aſhore, and examin'd before the Governor; but we underſtood nothing of their Language, and could make him no Anſwer, till one Mr. *Gould*, a Linguiſt, was brought to us; and upon underſtanding our Caſe, the Governor clear'd us. But the Cruſidore, a ſort of Super-intendant over the Iſlands, whoſe Power was ſuperior to the Governors, refus'd to clear us, and put us in Goal, where we lay 24 Hours.

The next Day we were brought under Examination again, and then we
had

had for our Linguift one Mr. *John Curre*, who had formerly been in *New-England*. We gave them as full and diftinct Account as we could, where, and when, we were feverally taken, and how we had made our Efcape from the Pirates. They brought feveral Witnefies (*Portugueze*) againft us, as that we had taken them, and had perfonally been active in the Caption and Abufe of them, which yet they agreed not in; only they generally agreed that they heard fome of us curfe the Virgin *Mary*, upon which the Crufidore would have condemned us all for Pirates. But the Governor, who thought we had acted the honeft Part, interpos'd on our Behalf, and faid, that it was very plain, That if thefe Men had been Pirates, they had no need to have left *Low*, and under fuch Circumftances, and come in here, and refign themfelves, as they did; they could have ftaid with their old Companions, and have been eafily enough fupply'd with what they wanted; whereas their taking the firft Opportunity to get away from their Commander, and fo poorly accommodated, was a Proof to him, that we had no piratical Defigns; and if he (the Crufidore) treated us at this Rate, it was

was the way to make us, and all that had the Unhappiness to fall into Pirates Hands, turn Pirates with them. Yet all he could say would not wholly save us from the angry Resentments of the Crusidore, who, we thought, was inflam'd by the *Portugueze* that was among us. So he committed us all to Prison again, me with three others to the Castle, the rest to another Prison at some considerable Distance off : And so much Pains was taken to swear us out of our Lives, that I altogether despair'd of escaping the Death of a Pirate; till a Gentleman, Capt. *Littleton*, (if I mistake not) told me it was not in their Power to hang us, and this comforted me a little.

In this Prison we lay for about four Months, where, at first, we had tolerable Allowance, of such as it was, for our Subsistence; but after three Months time they gave us only one Meal a-day, of Cabbage, Bread, and Water, boil'd together, which they call Soop. This very scanty Allowance put us out of Temper, and made us resolve, rather than starve, to break Prison, and make head against the *Portugueze*, and get some Victuals; for Hunger will break thro' Stone Walls. The Governor understanding

derstanding how we far'd, told the Crusidore that we should stay in his Prison
no longer, as the Castle peculiarly was ;
and greatly asserted our Cause, and
urg'd we might be set at Liberty ; but
the Crusidore would not hearken as yet
to the clearing us, tho' he was forc'd
to remove us from the Castle, to the
Prison in which our Comrades were,
where after they had allow'd us about
an Hour's Converse together, they put
us down into close Confinement ; tho'
our Allowance was a small Matter better than it had been.

Under all this Difficulty of Imprison-
ment, short Allowance, and hard-Fare,
false Witnesses, and Fear, lest I should
still have my Life taken from me, (when
I had flatter'd my self, that if I could
but once set Foot upon a Christian Shore,
I should be out of the Reach of Danger) I had a great many uneasy Reflec-
tions. I thought no body's Case was
so hard as mine ; first to be taken by
the Pirates, and threaten'd with Death
for not joining with them ; to be forced away, and suffer many a drubbing
Bout among them for not doing as they
would have me ; to be in Fears of Death
for being among them, if we should be
taken by any superior Force ; and now
that

that I had defignedly, and with Joy, made my Efcape from them, to be imprifon'd, and threaten'd with the Halter. Thought I, When can a Man be fafe? he muft look for Death to be found among Pirates; and Death feems as threatning, if he efcapes from them. Where is the Juftice of this! It feem'd an exceeding Hardfhip to me. Yet it made me reflect, with Humility I hope, on the Juftice of GOD in fo punifhing of me for my Tranfgreffions; for tho' the tender Mercies of Man feem'd to be Cruelty, yet I could not but fee the Mercy and Goodnefs of GOD to me, not only in punifhing me lefs than I deferv'd, but in preferving me under many and fore Temptations, and at length delivering me out of the Pirates Hands: And I had fome Hopes that GOD would yet appear for me, and bring me out of my Diftrefs, and fet my Feet in a large Place.

I thought my Cafe was exceedingly like that of the Pfalmift, and the Meditation on fome Verfes in the XXXVth *Pfalm* was a peculiar Support to me: I thought I might fay with him, *Falfe Witneffes did rife up; they laid to my Charge things that I knew not; they rewarded me Evil for Good. But as for me, when*

they

they were taken, (tho' I don't remember
I had ever seen the Faces of any of
them then) *I humbled my self, and my*
Prayer returned into my own Bosom; I be-
hav'd my self as though they had been my
Friends; I bow'd down heavily, as one that
mourneth for his Mother; but in my Ad-
versity they rejoyced, and gather'd them-
selves together against me; yea, they open'd
their Mouth wide against me, — they gnash-
ed upon me with their Teeth, and said, aha,
aha, our Eye hath seen it; — so would we
have it.   But, Lord, how long wilt thou
look on? Preserve my Soul from their De-
struction; let not them that are mine Ene-
mies wrongfully rejoyce over me; — stir up
thy self, and awake to my Judgment, even
unto my Cause, my God, and my Lord, and
let them not rejoyce over me, — and I will
give thee thanks in the great Congregation,
my Tongue shall speak of thy Righteousness,
and thy Praise, all the Day long.

In the midst of all my other Calami-
ties, after I had been in this Prison a-
bout two Months, I was taken down
with the Small-pox, and this to be sure
was a very great Addition to my Misery. I knew well how we dreaded this
Distemper in my own Country, and,
thought I, how can I possibly escape
with Life? To be seiz'd with it in a

I   Prison,

Prison, where I had no Help, no Phyfician, nor any Provision fuitable thereto; only upon my firft being taken I fent word of it to the Conful, who was fo kind as to fend fome Bundles of Straw for me to lie upon, inftead of the hard Stones, which as yet had been my Lodging, and the *Portugueze* gave me fome Brandy, and Wine and Water, to drive out the Pock. I was exceedingly dejected, and had nothing to do but to commit my felf to the Mercy of GOD, and prepare my felf for Death, which feem'd to have laid hold upon me; for which way foever I look'd, I could fee nothing but Death in fuch a Diftemper, under fuch Circumftances; and I could fee the *Portugueze* how they ftar'd upon me, look'd fad, and fhook their Heads; which told me their Apprehenfions, that I was a dead Man. Yet I had this Comfort, that it was better to die thus by the Hand of GOD, than to die a vile Death by the Hand of Man, as if I had been one of the worft of Malefactors.

But after all, it pleas'd GOD in His wonderful Goodnefs fo to order it, that the Pock came out well, and fill'd kindly, and then I had the Comfort of feeing fome of the *Portugueze* look more
pleafant

pleafant, and hearing them fay, in their Language, that it was a good fort. In about five or fix Days the Pock began to turn upon me, and then it made me very fick, and at times I was fomething out of order in my Head; and having no Tender or Watcher, I got up in the Night to the Pail of Water to drink, which at another time, and in another Place, would have been thought fatal to me; but GOD, infinite in Mercy, prevented my receiving any Hurt thereby, and rais'd me up from this Sicknefs.

After I recover'd of this Illnefs, I was but in a weak Condition for a long Time, having no other Nourifhment and Comfort, than what a Goal afforded, where I ftill lay for near three Months longer. At length, fometime in *June*, 1723, I was taken out of Goal, and had the Liberty of the Conful's Houfe given me, who treated me kindly, and did not fuffer me to want anything that was necefſary for my Support.

While I was at Liberty, I underſtood there was one *John Welſh*, an *Irifhman*, bound to *Lisbon*, whom I defir'd to carry me thither. And in the latter end of *June* I fet fail in him for *Lisbon*,

I 2   where

where we arriv'd about the middle of *July*, after we had been 21 Days upon the Paffage. When I had got to *Lisbon*, being almost naked, I apply'd my felf to the Envoy, told him my Condition, and defir'd him to beftow fome old Cloaths upon me. But he (good Man!) faid to me, that as I had run away from the Pirates, I might go to work for my Support, and provide my felf with Cloaths as well as I could And I found I muft do fo, for none would he give me. I had nothing againft Working, but I fhould have been glad to have been put into a working Garb; for I was fenfible it would be a confiderable while before I could purchafe me any Cloaths, becaufe *Welch* play'd me fuch an *Irifh* Trick, that he would not re-leafe me, unlefs I promis'd to give him the firft *Moidore* I got by my Labour; tho' I had wrought for him all the Paf-fage over, and he knew my poor Cir-cumftances: However, when I came to fail for *New-England*, *Welch* was better than his Word, and forgave me the *Moidore*, after I had been at the Labour of unloading his Veffel.

I fpent fome time in *Lisbon*; at length I heard there was one Capt. *Skille-gorne* bound to *New-England*, with whom

I

I took my Passage home; who cloathed me for my Labour in my Passage. We touch'd in at *Madera*, and arriv'd at *Boston* upon *Wednesday September* 25, 1723. and I at my Father's House in *Marble-Head* the *Saturday* after.

So has G O D been with me in six Troubles, and in seven. He has suffer'd no Evil to come nigh me. He has drawn me out of the Pit, redeem'd my Life from Destruction, and crown'd me with Loving-kindness and tender Mercies. Unto Him be the Glory for ever. Amen.

NICHOLAS MERRITT, *jun.*

GOD's Ability to save his People out of all their Dangers.

DAN. III. 17.

IF it be so, our GOD, whom we serve, is able to deliver us from the burning Fiery Furnace, and He will deliver us out of thine Hand, O King.

WE have here before us the remarkable History of what befel Three Young Men of the *Jews*, who were carry'd away captive by the *Chaldeans*, into *Babylon*. The haughty *Nebuchadnezzar* had caus'd an Image of wonderous

rous Stature to be made of Gold, and, pass'd a severe Decree, that all Men, upon hearing the musical Instruments, which he order'd to be founded at certain Times, should fall down and worship the golden Image, upon pain of their being cast into a Fiery Furnace. The three Jewish Worthies, *Shadrach, Meshach,* and *Abed-nego,* steadily adher'd to the Worship of the true GOD of *Israel,* the GOD of their Fathers, and, in Compliance with his Commands, abhor'd such gross Idolatry, and therefore, notwithstanding the heavy Penalty annexed to the *Persian* Edict, utterly refus'd to bow the Knee, and give any religious Worship to the golden Image which *Nebuchadnezzar* had set up. Some of the bigotted *Chaldeans,* observing that these three young Men neglected to comply with the King's Command, accus'd them to his Majesty of Contempt of his Royal Authority, and Breach of his Imperial Edict, saying, *ver.* 12. *These Men, O King, have not regarded thee, they serve not thy gods, nor worship the golden Image which thou hast set up.* Upon which *Nebuchadnezzar* was kindled into Fury, to think that any from among the poor Captives of the *Jews,* and these young Men, should dare to take upon them

to

to govern themſelves more by the Di-
ctates of their own Minds, inform'd by
the Law of the GOD of *Iſrael*, than by
his Royal Will and Pleaſure, and under the Pretence of Conſcience, refuſe
to obey his Command, which. enjoyned
the religious Worſhip of what he ac-
counted his God, on pain of his higheſt
Diſpleaſure; he immediately ſends for
them, and haſtily, and angrily queries
with them, for their audacious Contempt of him: *Is it true, O Shadrach,
Meſhach, and Abed-nego? Do ye not ſerve
my gods?* And he aſſures them, that if
they did not worſhip his gods, they
*ſhould be caſt the ſame Hour into the midſt
of a burning fiery Furnace.* Such a quick
Riddance was he reſolv'd to make of all
that dar'd to diſſent from his eſtabliſh-
ed Religion! And *who is that God* (ſaid
that haughty Monarch) *that ſhall deliver
you out of my hands?*

The three devout young Men anſwer
him with a truly heroick Spirit, and
Fortitude of Mind, becoming them as
Men, and as thoſe that fear'd the
LORD GOD of Heaven; *O Nebuchadnezzar,* ſaid they, *we are not careful to
anſwer Thee in this Matter;* as if they
had ſaid, Sir, we are in your Hands,
you may do with us what you pleaſe,

we

we are not much concern'd what out-
ward Torment you shall inflict upon us;
we are ready to suffer any Penalty, rather than renounce the True GOD,
and turn to the worshipping of Idols;
we have plac'd our Hope and Trust in
the Living JEHOVAH, and doubt not
His Protection and Favour; for, as in
my Text, *If it be so,* that is, if thou
shouldst cast us into the fiery Furnace,
yet, *our God whom we serve, is able to deliver us from the burning fiery Furnace, and
He will deliver us out of thine Hand, O
King; but if not,* (as it follows in the
next Verse) if our GOD do not see
Cause to deliver us out of the Furnace,
yet (such their Faith and Trust in
GOD, and Resolutions for His Service,
that they could say) *be it known unto thee,
O King, that we will* not *serve thy gods,
nor worship the golden Image, which thou hast
set up.* Such their Resolution, that
they had rather undergo any Death,
than wilfully sin against GOD; and
their Hope and Trust in Him was
grounded upon His Infinite and Almighty Power to help them, and His
Goodness and Mercy to them in the
Conclusion, whatever they were call'd
to suffer for His Sake.

From

From the Words I shall observe this general Truth, *viz.*

DOCT. *THAT GOD is able to deliver them that serve Him, from the greatest of Enemies and Dangers.*

What a signal Instance have we of the Power of G O D, and His Ability and Readiness to deliver them that serve Him, in these three Children of the Captivity, whose memorable Story is before us. The Answer of *Shadrach, Meshach,* and *Abed-nego,* put *Nebuchad-'nezzar* into such a Rage that he could not contain himself, *The Visage of his Countenance was chang'd,* he appear'd all Wrath and Fury; and that the Furnace might be like himself, and make a thorough Dispatch of them, *He commanded that they should heat the Furnace one seven times hotter than it was wont to be heated;* and left there should be any possible Way left for their Escape out of the vehemently heated Furnace, *He commanded the most mighty Men that were in his Army, to bind Shadrach, Meshach, and Abed-nego, and to cast them,* so bound in their Cloaths, *into the burning fiery Furnace;* and so overheated was the Furnace, that those that did the Office

of

of casting them into it, *were slain by the Flame of the Fire,* upon their Approach only to the Verge of it; and yet after all, see the wonderful Power and Goodness of GOD to them that serve Him, He is able to deliver, and He will deliver; for tho' *those three Men fell down bound into the Furnace,* yet God quenched the raging of the Fire, and suffer'd it not to hurt them, to the Astonishment of *Nebuchadnezzar,* and all about him, for while he sat to glut his Eyes with beholding how the Flame would consume those that dar'd to dispute his Authority, and disobey his Word, he is surpriz'd with the amazing Spectacle, that those whom he had cast bound into the midst of the Fire, were *loose, walking in the midst of the Fire,* without having receiv'd any Hurt, with a *Fourth* Person walking among them, the *Form of whom was like the Son of God.* Upon such an astonishing Sight *Nebuchadnezzar* is possess'd with some Awe and Dread of the GOD of *Shadrach, Meshach,* and *Abed-nego,* and a Veneration for their Persons; and now in Respect to them, he comes himself nearer to the Mouth of the Furnace, and calls upon them, *Ye Servants of the most High God, come forth, and come hither;* and in the

Presence

Prefence of all his Nobles came forth thefe three Men, *upon whofe Bodies the Fire had no Power, nor was an Hair of their Head cinged, neither were their Coats changed, nor the Smell of Fire had pafs'd on them.* The Account of which we have in the latter Part of the Chapter where my Text is.

A like notable Inftance of the Divine Power, to protect and deliver the Servants of GOD, we have in *Daniel,* another of the Children of the Captivity; the Hiftory of which we have in the VIth Chapter of *Daniel.*

Darius, the Emperor of *Perfia* and *Media,* had fet 120 Princes over his Kingdom, at the Head of whom he had plac'd three Prefidents, and made *Daniel,* a *Jewifh* Captive, Chief among them; which greatly excited the Indignation and Envy of the feveral Princes, to fee a Captive preferr'd before them; infomuch that they enter'd into a Combination to take him off; but knowing the King's Fondnefs for him, they faw it would be in vain for them to attempt to remove him out of the Way by their own Power, and therefore they more politickly cover'd their malicious Defigns, and narrowly watch'd all his Motions, that, if poffible, they might find

K   fome-somewhat whereof to accuse him to the King, of want of Fidelity, or Male-Administration. After a long Time of envious Observation, they find *Daniel* preserv'd a steady Allegiance to his Sovereign, and prudently manag'd the Affairs of Government committed to his Trust, so that there was no Hopes of their picking any Matter of just Accusation out of so wise and faithful a Servant; and therefore they have Recourse to a Stratagem which they doubted not would succeed to their Wish. They remember'd, that tho' *Daniel* was thus advanc'd in the Persian Court, yet he was born and educated in the *Jews* Religion, and was still a strict Worshiper of the GOD of *Israel*. This they were resolv'd to improve against him; and therefore, under the fair Pretence of doing a great Honour to their Sovereign, a Bill is brought in, and passes among them, *That whoever shall ask a Petition of any God, or Man, for thirty Days, save of King Darius, should be cast into the Den of Lions.* This they bring to the King, and pray his signing of it, that it may pass into a *firm Decree, according to the Law of the* Medes *and* Persians, *which altereth not.* The King was easily taken with the Flattery, and readily signs the

Bill

Bill. And now they thought themselves sure of the Prey; and should have this Pleasure added to their Revenges, to see their Royal Master, who so highly honour'd *Daniel*, as hastily pull him down and destroy him. They had not waited long before they find *Daniel*, according to his daily Custom, upon his Knees, praying and giving Thanks to the God of Heaven, notwithstanding the establish'd Decree; and now they run hastily to the King, and mind him of the Decree, and inform him that his Favourite *Daniel* despis'd his Authority, and contemn'd his Edict, and dar'd, notwithstanding the Severity of it, to make his Petition three times a-day. The King now saw himself caught in the Snare, and his faithful Servant *Daniel* likely to perish, and therefore in great Concern for him *he labour'd till the going down of the Sun, to deliver him* from their Rage, but all in vain, (so weak is the Power of earthly Monarchs) for the envious Courtiers are but so much the more enraged, the more the King pleaded to save him, and growing mad and insolent, say to him, *Know, O King, that the Law of the Medes and Persians is, that no Decree nor Statute, which the King establisheth, may be changed;* and thus at length they extort from

K 2   their

their Sovereign a Command, against his Will, *that Daniel should be cast into the Den of Lions.* And yet see how wonderously GOD deliver'd him. The King, who had pass'd the Night without Sleep, in a melancholy Reflection upon the Loss of so valuable a Servant, came very early the next Morning to the Den, and cry'd out, *O Daniel, Servant of the living God! is thy God, whom thou serveste continually, able to deliver thee from the Lions? Then Daniel* answer'd the King, and said, *O King, live for ever; My God hath sent his Angels, and hath shut the Lions Mouths, that they have* not *hurt me, so Daniel was taken up out of the Den, and no manner of Hurt was found upon him, because he believ'd in his God.*

In these Instances has GOD made His Power to be known, that He is able to deliver those that fear him; and so great an Enemy as *Nebuchadnezzar,* and so terrible a Danger as a sevenfold heated Furnace, could not prevent the Deliverance of the three Children; nor so many potent Adversaries as the Princes of *Persia,* and the Law in Conjunction with them, and so horrid a Danger as a Den of hungry Lions, could not make a Prey of *Daniel,* but GOD could, and did deliver those His
Servants

Servants out of the Hands of them all.

I will only a little further illustrate and confirm the doctrinal Truth, by mentioning a few things briefly, and then pass into the Improvement.

1. *All Power belongeth unto GOD, so that He is able to do whatsoever he pleaseth.* To GOD belongs the Power of Right and Authority to rule and govern his Creatures, and all their Actions; for they are all the Workmanship of his Hands. He is the great Creator, and therefore the most high Possessor, or Lord Proprietor of Heaven, and of Earth. *Psal* XCV. 3, 4, 5. *The Lord is a great God, and a great King above all gods; in his Hands are the deep Places of the Earth, the Strength of the Hills is his also; the Sea is his;* and the Reason is, *He made it, and His Hands formed the dry Land.*

But then GOD has an Infinity of Power or Strength to perform his Pleasure. Men may have a Right to rule, and yet may want Strength to defend themselves from a successful Invasion upon their Right, by a bold and more potent Usurper. But GOD has all Power in his own Hands, so that he is able to defend himself against the united

Force

Force of all Creatures, and to accomplish his Pleasure against all possible Opposition. Hence we read, *Job* IX. 19. *If I speak of strength, lo, He is strong;* and *ver.* 4. *He is mighty in strength.* So that whatever GOD wills to do, that he is able to do; that is to say, all that is possible to be done, and that not only by Means and Instruments, but by Almighty Power. When therefore at any time we read in the Scripture, that GOD cannot do so or so, it does not intend that there is any want of any, the least possible Measure or Degree of Power in GOD, but it means that the thing it self is impossible to be done, and that either from the Contradictoriness of the Nature of things, as a thing cannot be True, and False, at the same Time, and in the same Respect; or from the Contradictoriness of things to the Nature and Perfections of GOD. Hence 'tis said, that it is impossible for GOD to lie, because this is contrary to the Perfections of his Nature: But all that comes within the Verge of a Possibility, and that not to finite, but to infinite Power, that GOD is able to perform, for he is the Lord Almighty, and can any thing be too hard for the Almighty? How then would he be Almighty?

mighty? Tho' it be true, that God may
not, or rather will not, do all that is
poffible to be done, yet the Reafon of
this is to be fetch'd from his own Sovereign Will and Pleafure, which is un-
controulable by any thing out of himfelf; for whatfoever he willeth to do,
he has Power fufficient to enable him
to execute his Purpofe. So that the
Power and Ability of God is infinite,
nor can any thing fet Limits thereto but
his own Will. Hence he fays, *Ifa.* xlvi.
10. *My counfel fhall ftand, I will do all my
pleafure.*

2. Hence, *GOD is able to over-rule all
the Enemies of his Servants, and prevent the
Dangers that threaten them.* For feeing
the Power of God is infinite, it is con-
fequently extenfive over all things; the
Hofts of Heaven, Earth and Sea, are
at his Command, and he is an over-
match for their united Strength. This
Nebuchadnezzar acknowledges, when he
faw how wonderfully God had deliver'd
the three Children out of his Hands,
and from the Violence of the Fire,
Dan III. 29. *I make a decree,* fays he,
*that every people and nation, and language,
which fpeak any thing amifs againft the God
of Shadrach, Mefhach, and Abed-nego, fhall
be cut in pieces, and their Houfes fhall be*

3   *made*

made a dunghill, becauſe there is no other God that can deliver after this ſort.

Yea, God has the Hearts as well as the Hands of all Men under his Government, and can turn them as he pleaſes; *Prov.* XXI. 1. *The king's heart is in the hand of the Lord, as the rivers of Water, He turneth it whitherſoever he will.* God has the Hearts of the greateſt and mightieſt of Men in his Cuſtody, they are at his Diſpoſal, he governs them by his Power, and can turn them at his Pleaſure; ſo that when they ſet themſelves to do Miſchief unto his Servants, he can lay Reſtraints upon their Luſts and Paſſions; when they are full of Malice and Rage, he can prevent their Malice, and extinguiſh their Rage, and make them to ſhew Acts of Kindneſs, inſtead of doing Hurt to them that ſerve him. Thus when *Eſau* came forth with an armed Band againſt *Jacob*, (moſt probably with Intentions to wreak his Revenges upon him) yet how ſoon did God over-rule him, that of an Enemy he became a Friend, and inſtead of hurting, offers, either with his whole Band to conduct him, that no Adverſary might annoy him, or at leaſt to leave ſome of his Forces with him, to aſſiſt him in driving

his

his Cattle, and in the carrying of his little ones and Goods. See *Genesis*, ch. XXXII and XXXIII.

Thus God is able to stay the Hands of their Enemies, when they are lifted up to smite them, or can wither them in a Moment. When a *Pharaoh* is set upon afflicting and vexing his People, and will not let them go to serve him, he is able to send his Plagues upon such an implacable Enemy, till he is glad to get rid of them, and hurry them away to the Service of their God: If he pursue after them with his armed Forces, purposing in his Rage to cut them off Root and Branch; all his mighty Power, with utmost seeming Advantages attending them, shall not be able to hurt them; for God is able to knock off his Chariot Wheels, and stop him in his Course; he is able to bring the Waters of the Sea, which parted, and stood up as a Wall for the safe Passage of his *Israel*, over *Pharaoh* and his *Egyptians*, and destroy them all in a Moment.

Thus God is able to over-rule the Dangers that threaten his Servants. Tho' threatning Dangers may be contingent to us, and we are not able to foresee and provide against them, yet God has the absolute Command of all

Contin-

Contingencies; they are all known unto him, and by his Power he rules and governs them as he pleases; or if the Dangers that threaten are the natural Result of second Causes, and we see them a coming, but can discern no possible Way of escaping them, yet GOD can over-rule second Causes, he can stop their Motions and Operations, suspend their Influences and Vigour, as he quenched the raging of the Fire, and stopped the Mouths of Lions; or he can give quite another Turn to them, he can cause the Sun to go backward, as well as to stand still on *Gibeon,* and by one or other is able to deliver them that serve him.

3. *GOD is able to establish and fulfil his Purpose against all the Counsels and Purposes of Men* For the Lord Almighty has none to stand in Competition with him, to equal and rival him in Power and Dominion, and therefore tho' the Enemies of his People look never so big, and swell never so much with Envy and Rage, though they enter into Combination and take Counsel together, project their Schemes never so nicely, and lay their Plots never so deep, yet all signifies nothing before the Arm of the mighty God of *Jacob;* for he is able to counter

counterwork their Defigns; as he can fpie out the hidden Works of Daikneſs, and difcover the (otherwife infcrutable) Devices in the Heart of Man, fo he is able to fruſtrate them, and bring them all to nought; He can take the Crafty in their own Craftineſs, and make them that feek the Hurt of his People to fall into the Pit which they have digged for them : *The Counfel of the Lord that ſhall ſtand, and the Thoughts of his Heart unto all generations,* Pfal. XXXIII. 11. And hence alfo the wife Man tells us, *Prov.* XIX. 21. *There are many devices in a man's heart; neverthelefs, the counfel of the Lord that ſhall ſtand.* In vain do any attempt to 'fet themfelves againſt the Purpofes of God; never any harden'd himfelf againſt God, and profper'd. Who is that God that ſhall deliver out of my Hands ? faid haughty *Nebuchadnezzar.* Vain Man ! how weak are thy Purpofes, when the Almighty meaneth not fo ? Tho' he refolv'd to confume the three Worthies in the feven - fold heated fiery Furnace, ſhall his Counfel ſtand ? No, the Lord of Hofts gives forth his Word, and the Fire lofeth its Power to hurt, and his Servants are delivered ; our God is able to deliver us. This *Nebuchadnezzar* himfelf is forced

ced to acknowledge, *Dan.* IV. 34, 35. *The moſt High, whoſe dominion is an everlaſting dominion.——He doth according to his will in the armies of Heaven, and among the inhabitants of the earth, and none can ſtay his hand, or ſay unto him, what doeſt Thou?* And thus *Darius* confeſſeth to the Glory of God, after *Daniel*'s Eſcape from the Lions Den, *Dan.* VI 26, 27 *He is the living God, and ſtedfaſt for ever, and his kingdom that which ſhall not be deſtroyed. —— He delivereth and reſcueth, and he worketh ſigns and wonders in Heaven, and in Earth.* In ſhort, God is irreſiſtible in his Counſels and Deſigns, and there is no controuling him in his Ways : *If he will work, who ſhall let him.* None ever ſucceeded in any miſchievous Intention to deſtroy any one Servant of God, when he meant to deliver him.

4. *'Tis eaſy with G O D to deliver his Servants from Enemies and Dangers.* Thoſe things that are hard and difficult to the united Force of all Creatures, are light and eaſy with God ; yea, that which is impoſſible to Creatures, as exceeding the utmoſt Reach of their Power and Strength, is no ways hard and difficult to the Almighty : As the Angel ſaid to *Abraham, Gen.* XVIII. 14. *Is any thing*

too hard for the Lord! He is the Lord Almighty, and can any thing be too hard for Almighty Power? It may be too hard for finite limited Power, but it can't be too hard for Almighty Power to deliver them that ſerve God, out of the extremeſt Dangers, and from the moſt potent Enemies. It was eaſy with God to create a World out of Nothing, He did but ſpeak the Word, Let there be ſuch a World, ſo and ſo modified, adorned and inhabited, and his Word is obeyed immediately : And how eaſy then is it with that God to whom creating Power belongs, to work Deliverance for his People? Here,

1. *How eaſily can GOD find out the proper Methods to deliver his Servants!* Tho' the Circumſtances of their Diſtreſs may be ſo peculiarly intricate and perplex'd, and the crafty Devices of their Enemies ſo hidden and encreas'd, that they can ſee no poſſible Way of their eſcaping, yet God can eaſily find out an unthought of Method, and in an untrodden Path, which no Vultur's Eye hath diſcover'd, to come and ſave them. When the Children of *Ammon, Moab,* and Mount *Seir,* combin'd againſt *Judah* in the Days of *Jehoſhaphat,* the

L weak

weak Powers of *Judah* were no ways
sufficient to cope with the superior
Force of their Enemies, nor could they
devise any politick Method, any Slight
or Stratagem, by which they could hope
to escape the Destruction that threat-
ned them: *We have no might against this
great company, that cometh against us, neither know we what to do*, say they; so
that they could see no Possibility of escaping, seeing they had neither Power
to withstand them, nor Art and Skill to
evade the coming Blow; and yet, when
their Eyes are to the Lord, and their
Hope and Trust is plac'd in him, how
easily does God find out a new and unthought of Method for their Deliverance, by setting their Adversaries at
Variance among themselves, till in the
Heat and Fury of their Jealousy and
Rage they had devour'd one another,
and left a rich and unguarded Camp
an easy Prey to the Men of *Judah*. The
History of which we have in the second
of *Chronicles*, Chap. XX. And thus,
when *Haman* was maliciously bent to revenge the Affront he thought he had receiv'd from *Mordecai*, not only upon
him personally, but all his Nation and
People with him, and had made the
Slaugh-

Slaughter of the *Jews* sure, as one would have been ready to think, by the Royal Edict devoting them to Destruction; what possible Way was there left (humanly speaking) for this poor, captivated, despised People, to escape the universal Desolation that was hastening upon them? and yet how wonderfully and unexpectedly did God find out a Way, in the very nick of Time, to involve *Haman* and his ten Sons in the Destruction designed for *Mordecai*, and those that confederated with him against the *Jews*, in the same Ruin that was design'd for them, while *Mordecai* and his People escap'd. See the History of it in the Book of *Esther*. Thus God can make the Stars to fight in their Courses, against his Peoples Enemies, and the Ordinances of Heaven to contribute to the Deliverance of his Servants.

2. *How easy is it with GOD to work Deliverance for his Servants, against, or without Means and Instruments!* Though GOD usually worketh by Means, yet he can go out of the ordinary Course of his Providence, and work contrary to them, or without them, as he pleases. GOD can go against the ordina-

ry Courſe of Nature, or the natural Operation of ſecond Cauſes, to fulfil his Deſigns, and bring about his Purpoſes. He that at firſt put thoſe Virtues and Powers into ſecond Cauſes, which they are endowed withal, can eaſily ſtrip them of their Efficacy, or put a new Vigour and Strength into them, which they naturally have not. How did he make the voracious Raven to part with his Food for the Support of his Servant *Elijah?* 1 *Kings* XVII. 4. How did he cauſe the Walls of *Jericho* to fall down at the Blaſt of Rams-Horns? *Joſ.* VI. 20 He is able to accompliſh Deliverance for his Servants, when there are no Means uſed, none that have a natural Operation to bring about ſuch an end: He can ſtretch forth his Arm, and is able, by the Strength of his own Right Hand, to pluck them as Brands out of the Burning, and reſcue them out of the Hands of them that hate 'em: He need but ſpeak the Word, and it ſhall be done. The Iron Gate will fly open of its own Accord, at the Command of GOD, to grant a Deliverance to his Servant *Peter* out of Priſon, *Aĉt* XII. 10. Theſe things ſufficiently illuſtrate and

and confirm this Truth, that G O D is able to deliver them that serve him.

I proceed to make some Improvement of what has been said.

1. Is GOD able to deliver them that serve him? *How terrible must the Thoughts of this be, to those that are at Enmity against God and his People.* Every wilful Sinner is an Enemy to God, *Rom.* VIII. 7. *The carnal mind is enmity against God, for it is not subject to the law of God.* The carnal Mind discovers its Enmity against GOD, in its want of Subjection to his Law, which is holy, just and good. Now, as God is able to deliver them that serve him out of the Hands of their Enemies, be they never so many and great, so he is able to inflict the deserved Punishment upon all that are in a State of Enmity against him; how truly terrible must it then needs be to the guilty Sinner, to think seriously of the Almighty Power of GOD? Well may it make his Flesh tremble, and his Heart to melt in the midst of his Bowels, to think what an Enemy he hath stirr'd up, and what an Avenger is in Pursuit after him. For though he

now

now mocks at Fear, and laughs at the Sound of the Threatning, though he rusheth on as into the Battle against the Almighty, trampling upon the Authority, and violating the Laws of God, yet let him know, and be assur'd of it, that he does but run upon the thick Bosses of the Buckler of the Almighty, to his own utter Ruin and Confusion; for all his Efforts shall not be able to weaken the Divine Arm, nor his collected Strength to stay the Hand of the most High, when it is lifted up to smite him. Earthly Monarchs may want Power to punish a bold Offender, and a Combination of Rebels may be too strong for them; a *David* may complain, *These sons of Zerviah are too hard for me*; but GOD cannot want Power to punish the greatest and most daring Sinner, nor can the Combination of all the Wicked of the Earth prevail against him. As he shews himself strong on the Behalf of those whose Hearts are perfect towards him, to accomplish Deliverance for them, so he will make his Power to be known on the Vessels of his Wrath, in the Day when he shall arise to execute Vengeance upon the Wicked, and Punishment upon the
People

People that difobey his Laws. How miferable then muft the Condition of the Wicked of the Earth be, who have this ftrong and all powerful GOD for their Enemy; for it is utterly impoffible for them to efcape, in the Day when He will execute his Wrath upon them, and pour out his Anger like Fire: *There is none can deliver out of his hand,* Job X. 7. When a *Nebuchadnezzar* fhall caft a Servant of GOD into a fiery Furnace, he may vauntingly fay, *Who is that God that fhall deliver out of my hands?* and yet our God is able to deliver them that ferve him, from his Rage and Cruelty; but when God himfelf fhall caft the Wicked of the Earth into Hell, moft intenfly heated by his fierce Indignation and Wrath, and where the Flame is inextinguifhable, there is none in Earth or Heaven that fhall be able to deliver out of his Hands. O what are poor Potfherds of the Earth, Worms of the Duft, that they fhould vainly imagine, that they can ftand it out againft that GOD, who fitteth on the Circle of the Heavens, and before Whom, all Nations are but as Grafhoppers; GOD will make them to feel the Effects of
his

his Power and Wrath in Hell, who will go on in Contempt of him and his Laws. And this will make Hell to be moft terrible, that there is the Wrath of an Almighty, which burns with moft amazing Fierceneſs, accompany'd with infinite Strength and Power, to hold the guilty Creature in endleſs Durance, and fix him irrevocably in the Place of Torment, beyond a Poſſibility of eſcaping. Wrath without Power might poſſibly be evaded, but where there is an Infinity of Power in Conjunction with inexpreſſible Wrath, how unavoidable is the Puniſhment? how exquiſite and interminable muſt the Miſery needs be? Verily, *'Tis a fearful thing to fall into the Hands of the Living God!*

And I might add; this Doctrine looks terribly upon the Enemies of GOD's Servants, they that hate them, and perſecute them for Righteouſneſs Sake, would do well to conſider, that the God that is able to deliver his Servants, is able alſo to avenge their Blood, and retaliate all the Miſchief and Spite of their Adverſaries; he can lift up himſelf, as Judge of the Earth, and render

a

a Reward unto the Proud; and great
Reafon have they to fear that he will
do fo.   But I pafs to fay,

2. This Doctrine may ferve to teach
us, *That we fhould not fear Man, but God.*
For if G O D is able to deliver them
that ferve him out of the Hands of the
moft powerful Enemies, then there is
but little Reafon why we fhould fear
Man, who, if G O D pleafe, fhall not
be able to do us the leaft Hurt; but
there is all imaginable Reafon for us to
fear GOD, left he fhould become our
Enemy, and give us up to the Will of
thofe that plot Mifchief againft us.

1. *This teaches us not to fear Man.*   I
do not mean, that we fhould not maintain fuch a cautionary Fear of Man, as
fhall put us upon our guard, left we
give any juft Occafion of Offence to
any, and fuch a reverential Fear of Man
as fhall excite us to pay the civil Honours
and Refpects that are due to every one
in their feveral Stations and Relations;
but that we ought not fo to fear Man, as
from the Apprehenfions of what they
may do to us, to be influenc'd to any thing
that is contrary to the known Laws of
GOD.

GOD. For the Will and Power of Man is limited, and bounded by the infinitely fuperior Will and Power of GOD, who brings Princes to nothing, and maketh the Judges of the Earth Vanity. Ceafe then from Man, for how unreafonable is it that he fhould be feared, whofe Breath is in his Noftrils, his Breath goeth forth, he dieth, and that very Day all his Thoughts perifh: All his Thoughts of Evil againft us ceafe with his Breath; and what Hurt then can he do unto us! Surely no Fear of Man fhould move us at any time to neglect a known Duty, but we fhould ftill attend our Duty, let who will threaten, and leave it with GOD to preferve us: *Daniel* did fo. Nor fhould any Fear of Man drive us to do a finful Action, but we fhould refolve with our felves not to comply with the Defire or Command of any to commit Sin, though it fhould be enforc'd upon us with the heavieft temporal Penalty: The Three Children did fo. For tho' Men may threaten us, what they will do unto us, yet they are not able to accomplifh their Threatning, but our GOD can quench the Fire of the Furnace, and the Fire of the Piftol levell'd

at

at our Heads or Breasts; he can turn away the Sword from us, can stay the Hand that is lifted up to smite us, and wither the Arm in a Moment that seems resolv'd to destroy, if we will not do such or such a wicked thing: Why then should we fear what Man can do unto us! Hence said GOD by his Prophet, *Isa.* LI. 12, 13. *Who art thou, that thou shouldest be afraid of a man, that shall die, and of the son of man, which shall be made as grass; and forgettest the Lord thy Maker, that hath stretch'd forth the Heavens, and laid the foundations of the Earth; and hast feared continually every day, because of the fury of the oppressor, as if he were ready to destroy? and where is the fury of the oppressor?* How should this Thought arm our Sea-faring Brethren and Neighbours particularly, with Resolutions not to fear Man, if at any time they fall into the Hands of the Sons of Violence, who not only entice, but threaten a present Death, in case of a Refusal to comply with them, in their impious and unrighteous Ways! You have seen that our God is able to deliver.

2 *This should teach us to fear* GOD. If GOD be able to deliver his Ser-

3   vants,

vants, then we should fear the Lord and his Goodness, that when we are endanger'd, we may experience his kind Protection. He is as able to kill and destroy, as to deliver and save alive, and therefore should we fear him ; yea, he is able to destroy not only our Bodies, but our Souls too in Hell for ever : How greatly then is he to be feared ? Thus Our SAVIOUR argues, *Mat.* X. 28. *Fear not them which kill the body, but are not able to kill the soul ; but rather fear him which is able to destroy both soul and body in hell.* The Lord is a great God, and a great King above all Gods, his Name is dreadful ; he can give a Commission to, and arm the least of his Creatures to hurt and destroy us ; he has innumerable Ways to destroy, as well as to deliver ; and the same mighty Power that can preserve us, can also bring us to the Dust of the Earth ; therefore should we stand in awe of him, and not Sin. Hence says the Prophet, *Jer.* X. 6, 7. *Forasmuch as there is none like unto thee, O Lord, Thou art great, and thy Name is great in Might, who will not fear thee, O King of Nations ? for to thee doth it appertain.* And thus we find *Darius* , after the signal Deliverance

wrought

wrought for *Daniel,* iffuing his Royal Proclamation in fuch Terms, *Dan.* VI. 26. *I make a Decree, that in every Dominion of my Kingdom Men tremble and fear before the God of* Daniel; *for he is the living God, and ftedfaft for ever.*

But,

3. *This teaches us to put our Truft in God.* Our God is able to deliver: To whom then fhould we repair for Shelter in an evil Day, but unto the Lord our God, whofe Name is a ftrong Tower, whereunto the Righteous run, and are fafe! The Ability of God to help us is the Foundation of our Truft: Ifa. XXVI. 4. *Truft ye in the Lord for ever, for in the Lord J E H O V A H is everlafting Strength.* The Power of God fhould encourage us to truft in him at all times, in all our Straits and Difficulties. He is able to fupply all our Wants for us, therefore fhould we not doubt his Power, or fay with incredulous *Ifrael* of old, *Can the Lord fpread a Table for us in the Wildernefs? Can he give us Bread and Flefh to eat?* But we fhould make known our Wants to him, and leave it with him to carve out for us what Portion of thefe things he

M   pleafes,

pleafes. He is able to deliver us from our Fears; therefore at what Time we are afraid, we fhould place our Truft in him, and recall our fainting Spirits in the Language of the Pfalmift, *Why art thou caft down, O my Soul? Hope thou in God.* He is able to bring us out of all our Diftreffes; therefore let our Cafe look never fo defperate, we fhould guard againft all Defpondency, and all finful Compliances with the Entice-ments of wicked Men, and caft our Burden upon the Lord, who is a pre-fent Help in Times of Trouble. Thus fay the three Children, *He is able——and he will deliver us*; fuch is their Con-fidence, Hope, and Truft in God. And we fhould learn to truft in God, when we have only his almighty Power to re-ly upon; I mean, when we can fee no likely human Methods to procure us what we want, or work Deliverance for us. What poffible Ground for Hope and Truft had the three Children from Men and Means, when caft into the fiery Furnace? Where could they look among all the Creatures of God, and fee the leaft Glimmerings of Hope to efcape the Violence of the Flame? But when all Hope and Help fails us

from

from the Creature, yet still we have the infinite Power of God to betake our selves to; he is then able to save us, and bestow the Blessing upon us. Thus to have our Hope and Trust placed in God, as able to deliver and help us, will be the most likely Way to preserve the inward Peace of our own Minds, and make us all calm and sedate within, when all things without us are thrown into Tempest and Confusion. For *happy is he whose Hope is in the Lord his God, which made Heaven and Earth, the Sea, and all that therein is;* Psal. CXLVI. 1. *He will keep him in perfect Peace, whose Mind is stayed on him, because he trusteth in him;* Isa. XXVI. 3.

4. *This should teach us to become the true Servants of God.* Our God, whom we serve, is able to deliver us, say they. But if we are not the sincere Servants of God, we can have no good Grounds to hope, that he will make bare his Arm, and shew us his Salvation : For God is angry with the Wicked every Ͱ , and those that walk in Disobedience to him, and trample upon his Laws, have reason to fear lest his

Power

pleases. He is able to deliver us from our Fears; therefore at what Time we are afraid, we should place our Trust in him, and recall our fainting Spirits in the Language of the Psalmist, *Why art thou cast down, O my Soul? Hope thou in God.* He is able to bring us out of all our Distresses; therefore let our Case look never so desperate, we should guard against all Despondency, and all sinful Compliances with the Entice-ments of wicked Men, and cast our Burden upon the Lord, who is a pre-sent Help in Times of Trouble. Thus say the three Children, *He is able——and he will deliver us;* such is their Con-fidence, Hope, and Trust in God. And we should learn to trust in God, when we have only his almighty Power to re-ly upon; I mean, when we can see no likely human Methods to procure us what we want, or work Deliverance for us. What possible Ground for Hope and Trust had the three Children from Men and Means, when cast into the fiery Furnace? Where could they look among all the Creatures of God, and see the least Glimmerings of Hope to escape the Violence of the Flame? But when all Hope and Help fails us

from

from the Creature, yet still we have the infinite Power of God to betake our selves to ; he is then able to save us, and bestow the Blessing upon us. Thus to have our Hope and Trust placed in God, as able to deliver and help us, will be the most likely Way to preserve the inward Peace of our own Minds, and make us all calm and sedate within, when all things without us are thrown into Tempest and Confusion. For *happy is he whose Hope is in the Lord his God, which made Heaven and Earth, the Sea, and all that therein is ;* Psal. CXLVI. 1. *He will keep him in perfect Peace, whose Mind is stayed on him, because he trusteth in him ;* Isa. XXVI. 3.

4. *This should teach us to become the true Servants of God.* Our God, whom we serve, is able to deliver us, say they. But if we are not the sincere Servants of God, we can have no good Grounds to hope, that he will make bare his Arm, and shew us his Salvation : For God is angry with the Wicked every Y , and those that walk in Disobedience to him, and trample upon his Laws, have reason to fear lest his

Power

Power should be manifested in inflicting very heavy Judgments upon them, and the worst that they feel in this Life, be but the Beginning of Sorrows to them ; but the Lord taketh Pleasure in the Prosperity of his Servants, and is ready to gird himself with Strength, and come and save them. This Consideration then should excite us to become the sincere and faithful Servants of the Most High God ; this should put us all upon a serious devoting of our selves to his Service, and a fixed Resolution to employ all our Powers for him, that we may glorify him with our Bodies and our Spirits, which are the Lord's. This should make us exceeding careful to approve and do the good, perfect, acceptable Will of God, that we may walk in all Well-peasing before him. This should make us to delight ourselves in his Law, to esteem his Precepts concerning all things to be right, and to hate every false Way. This should make us frequent, earnest, and importunate in our Prayers to God, that we may honour him in an Acknowledgment of our Dependance upon him. This should make us diligent, serious, and devout in our Attendance upon
the

the publick Duties of Religion in the House and Ordinances of our God. This fhould put us upon an hearty and unreferved Dedication of our felves to God in Chrift Jefus, choofing this God for our God, this Redeemer for our Saviour, upon his own Terms, and in his own Way. This fhould make us ready to lay our felves out in the Service of Chrift, being willing to fpend and be fpent for him, and to do all we can for the Honour of the Name of Chrift, and the Intereft of his Kingdom in the World. Yea, this fhould make us willing to fuffer any thing, to undergo any Hardfhips, to be expofed to any Death rather than to fin againft God. Thus fhould we become the true Servants of God, and then may we quietly hope and patiently wait for the Salvation of God.

Laftly. Has God at any time granted Deliverance to us? *Let us then give unto the Lord the Glory.* All our Deliverances of every kind come from God, who is the God of Salvation, and therefore unto him fhould we afcribe the Glory. Thus, Has God wrought Deliverance for us, when in a Time of

Sicknefs

Sickness he has preserved us from the noisome Pestilence, or raised us up when we were brought low? Has God delivered us from Shipwrack in Times of Storm and Tempest, and stilled the proud Waves of the Sea for us, and brought us to our desired Haven? Has he preserved us from falling a Prey into the Hands of barbarous Enemies, when we have been greatly endangered by them, or delivered us from Captivity to them that hated us? And especially, Has he rescued any of us from the Hands of Pirates, those evil and bloody Men, where our Life has hung continually in Doubt, and the Snares of Death have compassed us, and our better Interest has been in the utmost Danger of being lost for ever? Upon all such Deliverances let us call upon our Souls, and all that is within us, to bless his holy Name. See then the Hand of God in accomplishing all for us, acknowledge and praise his Power and Goodness to us in all. Let our glad Hearts adore him, while with our Lips we speak well of his Name, and in our Lives we endeavour to make Returns answerable to the Benefits we have received; and carefully pay our Vows

Vows to the Lord, which our Mouth hath uttered, or Heart purposed in the Day of our Distress. Thus we find *Jonah* after his signal Deliverance, as from the Belly of Hell, saying, *I will sacrifice unto thee with the Voice of Thanksgiving; I will pay that I have vowed; Salvation is of the Lord.* Jonah II. 9.

And now suffer me to address my self particularly to that young Man, who is here before the Lord this Day our Wonder and our Joy.

My dear Child,

We stand amazed at what God has done for you, and receive you as a Monument of the Divine Power, and a Miracle of Mercy. We are lost in the Meditation on the Wonders and Triumphs of the Power and Goodness of God to you. In you we see, that our God whom we serve is able to deliver out of the fiery Furnace, and from the Den of Lions. In you we see, that nothing is too hard for the Lord, and that 'tis not in vain for us to call upon him. In you we see, that there is room for us to trust to the Arm of the strong God to help us, when there is not the least rational Prospect from the Creature. In you we see, that 'tis safest

running

running the Risque of incurring the utmost Rage and Fury of Men, by denying all sinful Compliances with them, rather than to provoke God by joining with them in their pernicious Ways.

We cannot but hope, that there were some Dispositions in you to serve God before you were carried away Captive by a Crew of Pirates, almost three Years ago; and allow me to say, basely ungrateful, and deeply guilty beyond almost any Man in the World will you be, if now you do not become one of the most humble, holy, faithful, active Servants of God. To you therefore let my Counsel be acceptable this Day.

1. *Seriously reflect on the Wonders that God has wrought for you.* Often call to Mind the amazing Instances of the Goodness and Power of God, which you have had Experience of while you have been a Captive and an Anchorite; and as you call them to Mind, and have Opportunity, pen them down, that you may always have them by you, your Monitor and your Encouragement.

Particularly,

1. *Think what God has delivered you.*
from.

from. Think what Society you are freed from, such as you and we juftly efteem the worft of Men upon all accounts; Men of a fierce Countenance and Temper, full of Malice, Rage and Blood, with whom the almoft conftant noify Revellings, and perpetual Din of Madnefs, banifhed every focial Virtue, and rendered you confined to an Herd of Wild Beafts; among whom alfo the prodigious Defiances of Heaven, and amazing Affurances of their own Damnation (were it not that I might add Drunkennefs to their other Vices) gave you the livelieft Picture of Hell, and rendered your Companions no better than Devils incarnate.

Think alfo how many have been the Deaths you have efcaped. You have been in Perils by Water, in Perils by Land, and in Deaths oft; more, it may be, than your preferved Friend, whom we received with Joy fometime ago. Think how God preferved you, by reftraining the bloody Men from laying violent Hands upon you, when you fo often refufed to join with them in their evil Courfes; how you efcaped being taken a fecond time and fuffering Death, by your being providentially removed a little Diftance from fuch

as

as had been your Companions for a while ; how God delivered you when you were as a Mark set up to shoot at, and though the Bullets flew thick around you, yet none of them were suffered to harm you ; how you have escaped the Dangers that threatened you from the venomous Beasts of the Land, and the devouring Monsters of the Sea.

Call to mind the signal Care of God manifested to you, while you were alone in a desolate uninhabited Island for about nine Months together ; and that when you were just ready to perish under your Weakness and Wounds, and the great Rains of the approaching Winter, how marvellously did God send a Man to you, as it were an Angel from Heaven, to help you in your Extremity to Firing, and some other Necessaries of Life, which you were destitute of ; and by which means you were better able to shift for a Living for near seven Months after, when you were again alone ; and after that unexpected Company came to take up their Abode with you, what Civilities God moved them to shew to you.

2. *Think upon the Manner of your Deliverance.* The Manner of your Deliverance

verance has been filled with wonderful
Interpofitions of Divine Providence ;
and you may plainly fee, that nothing
fhort of the Arm of God, which alone
doth marvellous Things without Number, has wrought Salvation for you.
Whence elfe is it, that the Fire of the
Piftol, levelled at your Head, fhould be
three times going, extinguifhed, but
readily enough kindled into a Dif-
charge, when the fourth time its Aim
was directed from you.

How ftrangely were Matters over-
ruled for your firft going afhoar, when
the Chieftain of that mad Crew you
were among had fo often fwore you
fhould never go till he did ! His Revellings on Shoar proves the Means of
your Efcape.

And when you had taken a fmall
Tour, from the more conftant Place of
your Refidence, with two or three of
thofe Companions that had lately come
to you to another Ifland, at a fmall Diftance off, what a Sheltering of you was
this from the Fury of unreafonable
Men, who would undoubtedly have deftroyed you, at the fame time they
took the Refidue of your Companions.

And at laft, what a plain Interpofi-
tion of Providence was it, that by a
mighty

mighty and contrary Wind, those Vessels should be driven near to your desolate Habitation, and by the Want of Water, be put upon sending into your Harbour, in which you had an Opportunity of returning from your Captivity and Banishment, to your native Land? Truly 'tis the Lord's Doings, and it is marvelous in our Eyes.

2. *And now pay your Acknowledgments to GOD, by speaking and living to his Praise.* Surely you ought to speak well of the Name of GOD, and praise his Power, tell of all his Wonders which you have seen, utter the Memory of his great Goodness, and sing his Praise. Let nothing ever proceed out of your Lips that shall cast the least Dishonour upon the Name of G O D, but remember *Nebuchadnezzar*'s Decree after the Deliverance of the Three Children, *Dan.* III. 29. *I make a decree,* says he, *That every People, Nation and Language, which speak any thing amiss against the G O D of Shadrach, &c. shall be cut in pieces, and their houses shall be made a dunghill;* so spake natural Conscience; and in it you see what they deserve that blaspheme the Name of GOD.

G O D has preserv'd your Soul in Life, by his kind Visitation, now give him

3

him the Praiſe by living to his Glory. We doubt not but you have often call'd upon the Name of the Lord, (we alſo have lifted up our Cry to GOD on your Behalf) the Lord hath heard the Voice of your Supplication, your Groaning hath come up before him, and he hath ſent forth his Word, and drawn you out of the Pit, and redeemed you from the Hand of your Enemies, and from a ſtrange Land, and turned your Captivity, as the Streams of the South, to the unexpected Refreſhment of the weary Soul; and now it becomes you to live a Life of Thankfulneſs, in a grateful Obedience to all the Commands of GOD, reſpecting your Maker, and your Fellow-Creatures; that by exerciſing your ſelf always to have a Conſcience void of Offence both towards GOD, and towards Man, you may ſhew forth a lively Inſtance of the Grace of GOD, as well as be a Monument of his Power; that Praiſe may redound unto the Name of GOD, in the Churches, by the Thankſgiving of many on your Behalf.

Wherefore watch againſt all Sin, even the leaſt, and thoſe eſpecially which your Age and Company may moſt of all addict you to, and be not drawn a-

N way

way by the evil Example and Entice-
ments of others.

Take the Word of G O D for the
Rule of your Walk, and let it be your
Care daily to read it, serioufly to me-
ditate on it, and govern your felf in
your whole Deportment by it, that or-
dering your Steps according to that
Word, your Way may be cleanfed,
your Path may be fhining, and your
Walk pleafant.

Let the Deliverance of your Body
lead you to Jefus Chrift, to perfect
Redemption for your Soul; fee your
felf in an undone, miferable State and
Condition while a Stranger to him, and
a Captive to Sin, Satan and the World,
and earneftly cry to him for Help, and
fubject your felf to him, according to
the Laws of the Gofpel, cafting your
Soul upon him, relying upon him alone
for Righteoufnefs and Salvation, and following of him in the Regeneration ; and
by a holy Life let all Men fee, that you
are truly his Servant, who hath loofec
your Bonds.

While you were alone for fo many
Months, you had a long and peculia
Time to converfe with GOD, and you
own Soul, and every Day was as a Sab
bat

bath to you, wherein your Thoughts were chiefly reſtrained to GOD and Nature; let it now be your Care to maintain an holy Walk with GOD, in your daily Converſe with him in the Duties of Religion, and devoutly ſanctify the Lord's Day, as a ſpecial Day of Reſt and Rejoycing to you, both upon a ſpiritual and temporal Account. I will only further commend to you two or three Texts of Scripture for your ſerious Conſideration, *viz. Prov.* XIII. 20. *He that walketh with wiſe men ſhall be wiſe, but a companion of fools ſhall be deſtroyed.* Another Text is that, *Pſal.* CXVI. 12, 13, 14. *What ſhall I render unto the Lord for all his benefits towards me? I will take the cup of ſalvation and call upon the name of the Lord; I will pay my Vows unto the Lord.* — The laſt I ſhall mind you of is that, *Ezra* IX. 13, 14. *After all that is come upon us for our evil deeds, ſeeing thou our God haſt given us ſuch deliverance as this; ſhould we again break thy commandments, — wouldſt thou not be angry with us, till thou haſt conſumed us, ſo that there ſhould be no remnant or eſcaping?*

And O joyful Parents! (who have been in Anguiſh of Spirit for this your Son, and have travelled in Pain a ſecond

cond time for him, mourning in Bitterness of your Souls, becaufe this your *Joseph* was not) behold the Lord hath look'd upon you, he hath confider'd your Affliction, and turned again his Captivity, furprizing you with the unexpected, but joyful Acclamation, that this your Son, which was dead, is alive; he was loft, but is found. How were you like them that dream; when the Evening before the laft Lord's Day he unexpectedly came upon you, and brought the welcome Tidings of his Safety, and his Arrival among you And fhall not you alfo endeavour a more holy, watchful, fruitful Life and Converfation? Sure I am, GOD expects it from you. Well then, carefully render unto the Lord anfwerable to the diftinguifhing Benefits you have received from him; and unite in that Doxology, *Eph* III. 20, 21. *Now unto him that is able to do exceeding abundantly above all that we ask or think, according to the power that worketh in us, unto him be glory in the Church by Chrift Jefus, throughout all ages, world without end.* AMEN.

$$F\ I\ N\ I\ S.$$